Community Schools Partnership

PROJECT IMPACT REPORTS | 2018

United Way
Lower Mainland

Dialogues In Action
408 NW 12th Ave, Suite 506
Portland, OR 97209
503.329.4816
dialoguesinaction.com

Table of Contents

Introduction to the Project

The aim of Project Impact is to develop in nonprofits and public agencies the ability to do credible self-studies of their impact.[1] As such, this is a capacity-building project. A cohort of teams joined together from seven programs that are partners in the United Way of the Lower Mainland's Community Schools Partnership to go through this evaluation journey together. The reports in this compendium are written by the participating teams and represent the findings from their data collection and analysis.

The development of evaluation capacity takes time and iteration. It requires both instruction and practice – training in some of the leading techniques of research accompanied by ongoing applications and practice. This project recognizes the power of partnership, the enrichment of cross-pollination of ideas among like-minded organizations, the durable impact of a learning community, and the potential inspiration for a sector when exemplars are developed and elevated.

---

1   This project is primarily focused on developing the ability of staff teams to implement self-studies about the effects of their programs. It is not designed to provide an experimental or quasi-experimental version of impact evaluation. Instead, it is an effort to upgrade the existing capability of each organization and give them tools to gather data on their attributed impact both qualitatively and quantitatively from the subjects they serve.

Project Impact takes teams of leaders from nonprofits and public agencies through a process of discovery about the power of evaluation. The idea is to develop the ability to see and communicate the effects of the programs on the people they are designed to serve. There are three primary movements to the project: (1) Intended impact, (2) Inquiry, and (3) Implication.

Project Design

The project begins with a focus on the work of identifying and clarifying the intended impact of each of the participating programs. Once the ideas have been developed and indicators identified, the teams then design a questionnaire to collect data about quantitative measures and a qualitative interview protocol to collect qualitative data. These data are analyzed. Themes are identified and then translated into findings. From the findings, the teams develop program responses and communiques of their impact.

The fundamental elements of the Project Impact follow an arc of evaluation design:

Part 1 - Intended Impact

This project begins with the identification and clarification of what effects are intended through the work of each of the projects. Each team develops an articulation of intended impact to include the components necessary for evaluation design.

A. Main Ideas of Impact

Each team identifies and crafts ideas of impact to frame the intention of direct impact for the program. In some cases, these ideas are mapped in relation to the secondary and tertiary impacts of the program to gain clarity about the fundamental notions of desired effect as a direct consequence of the program or service rendered.

B. "What We Mean"

From these primary ideas, the teams then develop a brief explication of the meaning of their ideas of impact. This translates ideas that are occasionally technical into messages accessible to all.

C. Quantitative Indicators

Teams then identify quantitative indicators for each of the ideas. The aim is to generate five or six of the most critical indicators for each idea, paying attention to the data power, proxy power, and communication power of each of the key ideas. The intent in this step is to identify a range of cognitive, affective, and behavioral indicators that can be measured through metrics.

D. Qualitative Indicators

Teams also identify qualitative indicators in this stage. These indicators are articulations of the structural and qualitative elements of growth and development that signal progress toward key ideas of impact. The qualitative indicators become the basis for the protocol construction to inform the in-depth interviews in the inquiry phase.

2. Inquiry

In the inquiry stage of the project, each team designs and implements a strategy for data gathering. These take two forms: a questionnaire to collect quantitative data and an in-depth interview to gather qualitative data.

A. Quantitative Data and Analysis

For each of the quantitative indicators, teams construct items for a questionnaire. Since these projects are not intended to provide experimental or quasi-experimental inquiry, the attribution of effect is built into the questionnaire items. The questionnaire is deployed, in most cases, to the entire population of recipients the program reaches. Data are analyzed mostly using measures of central tendency. The teams then design displays of the data and narrative for their report.

B. Qualitative Data and Analysis

The development of a qualitative design encompasses a number of steps, including the following:

1. Protocol Design. Each team designs an in-depth interview protocol that uses the Heart Triangle™ method of question design. These produces a protocol of about nine sequences of questions (18 questions in total) to be used as a guide for seeking data about the awareness and reflection of subjects' structural shifts and developments of growth and progress.

2. Sample. Each team determines a sample of subjects using a purposeful stratified technique to identify a selection representative of the population being served.

3. Data Collection. Interviews are convened, most lasting between 45 minutes and 1 hour in length. Data are collected via notes during the interview, and then augmented immediately following the interview to provide a substantive rendering of the interview.

4. Data Analysis. Team members apply a four-step model of analysis to each of the interviews. This process provides them with a casual version of coding and interpretation, illuminating the primary themes from each interview.

5. Thematics. Through a guided and facilitative process, teams examine their entire data corpus. Themes are mapped through meta-analysis of the emerging insights and the most salient of them are brought forward as findings to be further described in a report and to inform future program development.

3. Implication

The intent of the project is not to leave teams simply with a report about their program's effects, but rather to use the insights from the evaluation to guide the further development of the program. This takes two forms:

A. Program Adjustments

The team then takes each of the findings from the evaluation and considers possible program adjustments informed by the discoveries of the evaluation. This keeps the evaluation relevant for program application and improvement.

B. Program Experiments

In addition, the teams work to identify potential design experiments that they might run as an implication of the insights gained through the evaluation.

In this stage, the teams also begin to develop a report of the evaluation findings as well as other possible communiques of their discoveries to staff, stakeholders, funders, and other members of the community.

Explanation of the Reports

The reports from the organizations in this cohort are included in the following compendium. These include highlights from the three movements of the Project Impact. For each participating organization, there is an explication of the primary findings from the evaluation accompanied by the programmatic responses of strategy and design. Since each organization has unique strategy and ethos, each report exhibits unique character and personality. Each report also includes both "prove" findings (evidence of impacts being achieved) and "improve" findings (areas for attention and further development). These reports are windows into the effects of the work of these organizations in the lives of the people they serve.

New Westminster Schools

Jumpsport

Rick Bloudell, Mattias Boon, Quirina Gamblen, Iain Lancaster

Organization and Program Overview

Organization

New Westminster Community Schools is a department within the New Westminster School District. The school district, as a whole, consists of 8 elementary schools, three middle schools, and one high school that serve a total of over 7500 students. New Westminster has two District Community School Coordinators who work with community partners to deliver subsidized after-school programming that builds student connection to schools and strengthen our students' success.

District Community School Coordinators spend a majority of their focus at two elementary schools. These schools have been determined to most benefit from the services, programs, and activities provided by Community Schools. Community Schools is about embracing change, being open to new ideas, methods, and processes. It is about greeting vulnerable children, youth and families with open arms and seeking out opportunities that will benefit individuals and the community as a whole. In partnership with the community, Community Schools provide individuals the means to make inspiring changes in their lives.

Program Description

Jumpsport has been a signature physical literacy program for Community Schools over the past five years. The program is offered three times per year for six weeks at a time. Jumpsport aims to teach students the fundamental movement skills that will allow them to be active for life. Students learn various skills, such as running, jumping, throwing, and catching, and then practice those skills through engaging activities. Jumpsport also exposes students to a variety of different sports, with one of the goals being to potentially spark an interest to pursue a certain sport in the future.

Canadian Tire Jumpstart Foundation is a funding partner for Jumpsport. They provide funding for students from low-income families to participate in the program free of charge.

The program also utilizes volunteers from both New Westminster Secondary School and Douglas College. New Westminster Community Schools has a valuable partnership with Douglas College Sports Science Department. Community Schools receives 2-3 students per semester who assist in leading the program as part of their fieldwork. This fieldwork is necessary for their graduation, and we have hired students after they have graduated as paid program staff.

The program's goals are to have the following impacts on students who participate in the program:

➤ Become physically active for life.
➤ Become empathetic towards their classmates and teachers...
➤ Become strong self-managers with high levels of emotional resiliency
➤ Will build healthy relationships with peers and caring adults

Evaluation Methodology

The aim of our evaluation was to see what kind and quality of impact the Jumpsport program is having at Lord Kelvin and Qayqayt Elementary School. To understand this, we explored two broad research questions:

➤ What kind and quality of impact are we having on students?
➤ What aspects of our program are causing this impact?

Over the course of the project, we (a) developed and refined our ideas of intended impact and indicators, (b) designed and implemented a mixed methods outcome evaluation using both qualitative and quantitative means to collect and analyze data, (c) identified findings, and (d) considered the implications to those findings for program improvement and innovation.

This project began with a focus on the work of identifying and clarifying the intended impact of the Jumpsport program. Once the ideas of impact had been developed, we used the Heart Triangle™ model to identify qualitative and quantitative indicators of impact focused on the mental, behavioral and emotional changes in students that indicate we are achieving our impact. We then used these indicators to design a qualitative interview protocol and a quantitative questionnaire to measure our progress toward achieving our intended impact.

Qualitative Data Collection and Analysis

For the qualitative portion of the evaluation, we designed an in-depth interview protocol to gain data about the structural, qualitative changes resulting from our program. We used a purposeful stratified sampling technique to select a representative sample from the population we serve. The population is defined as one parent or caregiver per student. Therefore, our population size was 53. Our sample size was 16, and we drew our sample from the following strata of our population:

> Parents

> Grandparents

> Foster Parents

Our interview team consisted of 2 District Community School Coordinators.

We then convened one-on-one interviews lasting from between 45 minutes and one hour in length with a sample from the identified strata of the population. Interviewers gathered the data by capturing the conversation through written notes during the interviews and filled in the notes immediately after the interview to obtain a substantive rendering of the interview.

We analyzed the data inductively using a modified version of thematic analysis. Interviewers implemented the first three phases of thematic analysis (becoming familiar with the data, generating initial codes and identifying themes) for each interview. The interviewers analyzed the raw data by reviewing each interview four times through each of four lenses to illuminate a different aspect of what the data reveal about the research question. The data were then gathered into four categories to serve as an initial set of codes. Then, intra-interview themes were generated based on the pervasive insights from the data. This process allowed us to interpret the meaning and significance of the data from each interview.

Next, we brought all of the data analyses and initial themes together and implemented the next two phases of thematic analysis (reviewing themes, defining and naming themes). We reviewed the initial themes as a team to identify the overarching and inter-interview themes that emerged from the full scope of our data analysis to illuminate the collective insights and discoveries. We mapped these themes visually and examined them in various ways to gain a greater definition of the features of the themes, causes, and catalysts of the themes, new or surprising insights related to the themes, and relationships between the themes that were revealed in the data. We then determined the most significant and meaningful discoveries and brought them forward as findings to be described in the final phase of thematic analysis, this report.

Quantitative Data and Analysis

For the quantitative portion of the evaluation, we designed a questionnaire to collect data on our quantitative indicators of impact. We administered this instrument to 53 parents and caregivers and had a response of 37 people, for a 69.8% response rate. The data were analyzed primarily using measures of central tendency. We identified key insights, patterns, and gaps within the data and incorporated these discoveries into the related findings.

Findings

Finding 1
Jumpsport staff are the single greatest factor for the program's success

Description
The most compelling theme resulting from parent and caregiver interviews is the impact program staff have had on students. It was vital to us that the program staff was not merely overseeing an open gym sports program. Program staff taught fundamental movement skills that students could build upon to learn and excel in other sports and activities. Parents and caregivers reported what one would expect from a program leader. They were routinely described as fair and positive role models. One parent gushed about her son's thoughts towards the leaders: "He likes the Jumpsport staff and volunteers. He gets positive reinforcement from them, and it allows him to build connections with adults." Program leaders were also credited with inspiring students to try new things and work with each other to ensure everyone is succeeding. A parent explained how her son had brought leadership skills home with him: "He tries to mediate situations and I think he learned that from the Jumpsport instructors and being in a team atmosphere." The magnitude of their leadership has far exceeded our expectations.

Parents and caregivers also recognize that the leaders genuinely enjoy spending time with students, including those with challenging behaviours. They are taught both physical skills and self-regulating techniques to help them gain resilience and confidence.

See chart on next page

Significance
Students have not always felt welcome around adults. Some students have been through adoption, while others have felt abandoned by one or both parents. Through a six-week program, these students have been

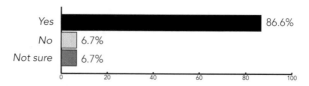

Figure 1. Percent of parents and caregivers who reported their child developed a trusting relationship with an adult from the program.

able to forge meaningful connections with Jumpsport staff and volunteers. This connection is the first step in order for students to benefit from the program.

Students must have a sense of belonging in order to succeed at school. The Jumpsport staff offer a welcoming atmosphere for an extremely diverse group of students. Once the students have arrived, they are engaged, and their confidence is continuously being built upon.

As Community School Coordinators, it is vital that we continue to ensure our staff feel supported and receive the necessary training. Since our Jumpsport staff and volunteers are students, coordinators must have a continuity plan in place to account for turnover when staff move on.

Responses

➢ Put more focus on Peer Leadership courses at New Westminster Secondary School

➢ Expose high school students to the following areas:
- mentoring younger students
- develop program organizational skills
- working with younger students with learning and physical challenges

➢ Connect staff more to the goals of the redesigned BC Curriculum, particularly to the core competencies of personal and social development

➢ Offer credit towards graduation for high school students who volunteer to lead programs

Finding 2

Friendships don't happen naturally for many students

Description

Jumpsport attempts to serve as a vehicle for students to make friends at school. It serves as a safe place for students to feel accepted and they are taught teamwork and skills necessary to build friendships. Despite school and program staff's best efforts, negative behaviour amongst peers still exists in classrooms, on the playground, and in programs. A number of parents reported their child facing struggles around others. One parent mentioned that "there is a lot of anxiety with current peer groups. Kids aren't always nice, and they can say really mean things that are difficult for me to hear. One student told her she was fat."

In addition to bullying, many students have anxiety about building relationships with their peers. Jumpsport staff are working on this issue and offering tools for students to make friends; however, it is still a work in progress. One parent described the difficulty her daughter has connecting on deeper levels with others: "She has a hard time making friends, especially ones that she really gets attached to… it usually takes her a while, and she doesn't know how to approach them."

The graph below demonstrates that most parents do not look at Jumpsport as a strong vehicle for their children making friendships. It is clear that more intentional work needs to be done to support students socially.

See chart on next page

Although students are struggling to make friends at school and in programs, Jumpsport has been successful in bringing students together that may not otherwise interact at school. The program serves as a clean slate for many students to interact and celebrate successes together. One parent, whose family immigrated to Canada within the last five years, said, "Before [Jumpsport], they weren't making friends. It was just the three [siblings] all the time."

Figure 2. Top reason for registering child for Jumpsport

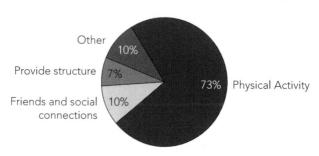

Significance

Anxiety around peers is pervasive for students. If students feel safe from ridicule and are confident in their abilities to make friends, school is going to be a more enjoyable experience for them. And if they are happy to be in school, they can focus on their learning rather than worrying about peers.

Parents reported that one reason that they appreciated Jumpsport is the fact that it gets their children away from their regular classmates and it offers an opportunity to meet new students. We, as Community School Coordinators, as well as program staff, may have assumed that once students are in the gym together, friendships will blossom naturally. It is clear that more intentional work needs to be done in this area. Jumpsport is going to work on providing the tools required for students to make friends. While this is occurring to some extent within the program, further work must be done to help students feel accepted and comfortable around each other.

Responses

- ➢ Work with public partners to find social spaces for children and youth
- ➢ Bring in a facilitator to work with staff on intentionally building friendship skills in students
- ➢ Offer parent education nights on the topic of social connections and friendships

Finding 3

Parents and their children: "What we've got here is a failure to communicate."

Description

Although the interviews have proven to be invaluable in gaining insight into the impact Jumpsport is having on its participants, they have also shed light on the fact that parents and caregivers are finding it difficult to communicate with their children. Evidence revealed that many students are coming home from school and are not wanting to share details about their day, despite questions from parents. This was especially true when it came to questions about emotions. A number of parents echoed similar responses, such as, "She is at that age where she doesn't like to talk about her feelings with me."

Alternatively, we learned many parents and caregivers are not asking their children questions about Jumpsport. Simply stated by one parent, "We don't talk about Jumpsport." This may indicate a much larger issue that spans beyond the program: are parents experiencing a challenge with work-life balance which is restricting the amount of time they can spend with their child? As one working parent said, "I just thought to start asking about the program on the way to school today." Other parents echoed similar sentiments about feeling the need to quiz their child about Jumpsport to prepare for their interview.

Significance

Whether it is the child who is not willing to open up or parents not approaching their child, it is evident that there is a disconnect and it should be addressed. It is common for students not to want to talk about their feelings. Program leaders, teachers, and school staff strive to work with students to peel back the layers and help them manage their emotions. These efforts must be continued at home.

Most parents and caregivers, undoubtedly, try to connect with their child, but they face obstacles. Some are limited due to work schedules, and therefore their child spends more time in childcare rather than the home environment. A lack of time spent together or potentially overlooking the importance of conversing about each other's day, is hurting communication efforts. Communication plays a vital role in students learning how to, and being able to, regulate their emotions. The Community School needs to and often does, serve as a resource for parents to connect with for assistance in helping their child.

Responses
- ➤ Invite parents to participate in Jumpsport
- ➤ Create inter-generational programs that encourage participation from both parents and children

Finding 4
Students are setting a foundation to be healthy for life

Description
Students are feeling better about themselves due to Jumpsport, but perhaps more importantly, they know why they are feeling better. Program staff has instilled the connection between physical health and mental well being. One parent has seen that "with exercise, she can better manage her feelings. She works off stress and overall feels much better about herself." Students understand how physical activity is connected to sleeping habits, reducing stress, and the need to eat healthy foods.

A mother, whose family moved to New Westminster in recent years, talked about the struggle with one of her children as he tries to adjust to the different types of food here: "He struggles with eating because there are a lot more fruits and vegetables in Canada than he is used to. I can't say that Jumpsport has solved the problem, but he is more willing to try new things because he knows that energy and food are connected."

Parents and caregivers also noticed that their child(ren) slept better on days that they attended Jumpsport or participated in other physical activity, and had fewer fights with siblings or other family members.

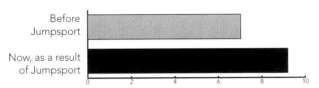

Figure 3. Change in number of hours of physical activity per week

The chart compares, on average, the number of hours per week that students spent participating in physical activity before and after attending Jumpsport. Of the 36 respondents, 77.78% reported an overall increase in the amount of physical activity. While this number is not surprising since we know their child is attending Jumpsport, and the program will account for at least 1-2 hours per week, a more positive indicator is that 46.64% of parents reported increases of more than 2 hours per week. This indicates that students are making lifestyle changes rather than just attending the program.

Significance

For children to become healthy and active adults, it is crucial that they begin participating in physical activity from an early age. Over 40% of students in New Westminster live in apartments (CNW Planning). In most cases, this drastically limits the opportunity and space for students to be active. Jumpsport provides an outlet for exercise in a fun and inclusive environment.

A student that is both physically and mentally healthier is going to be far happier and successful than one that is not. Students are taking initiative in their wellbeing. The fact that students are learning this at such a young age will hopefully set a foundation for the rest of their lives. This knowledge may prove to be Jumpsport's most significant and longest lasting impact on program participants.

Responses

➢ Utilize student surveys to elicit feedback and empower students to make their own healthy program choices

➤ Encourage more participation outside of school by promoting other organizations' programs, such as New Westminster Parks and Recreation

➤ Share our "pay what you can" registration model with other organizations to eliminate financial barriers

Finding 5

New-found physical skills are leading to confidence everywhere

Description

For many students, Jumpsport provides the only exposure to physical activity on a regular basis. Therefore, the onus is on the program to not only offer active play but also teach students basic physical skills. One mother reported significant improvements her daughter made throughout the six-week program: "I've seen her gross motor skills improve for sure. She can run better. Her hand-eye coordination has improved, and her stamina has gotten better than mine." Other parents have connected the stronger physical abilities to an increase in confidence for their children. One shared, "He has improved his coordination, and he is more willing to take on physical challenges." Another parent explained the struggles that her child has faced regarding body image issues and comments from other students. She reported, "There has been a slight change in strength, and she can feel it. Obviously, it's only a 6-week program, but her confidence in her athletic ability has increased."

Jumpsport's impacts are being felt beyond the gymnasiums. Student confidence is on display in the classroom and through the willingness to try new things. Parents have watched their children go from taking a passive to an active role when it comes to registering for programming. One parent was caught off guard by her daughter who was motivated to try a new sport that she learned in Jumpsport: "I registered her in community flag football because she knew she could do it. She wouldn't have done that in the past, but the confidence in her ability made her want to try." Children want to be more active in decisions that affect them.

Jumpsport instructors strive to instill a mindset on students that when they try hard and practice something, success will follow. The instructors hope that this mindset will translate to other areas of the students' lives. It is often a difficult concept for students to grasp; however, parents reported significant progress in the area. One parent expressed, "He would think he isn't good at anything. He's getting more confident. Today he spoke in front of his class." Another parent whose son has Attention Deficit Hyperactivity Disorder addressed his improvement around adults. She stated her son has a new-found "confidence in talking to [adults] and the ability to tell them exactly how something happens. He is more in control of his emotions around them too." On the quantitative survey, respondents reported that on a scale of one to five, children participating in the program experienced a significant increase in confidence, moving from an average of 3.92 to 4.46.

Significance

Students are developing fundamental physical skills that will give them the confidence to pursue sports and activities in the future. Sport for Life Society calls this the foundation for people to be "active for life." The increase in confidence in students from attending Jumpsport is extremely encouraging. In most cases, program staff can identify improvements in confidence within the program itself; however, parents are crediting Jumpsport for their children's increased self-esteem in the classroom and community. We believe that program staff is the leading cause for growing levels of confidence.

Our evidence is showing that students are feeling better about their physical abilities, communicating with adults, and expressing themselves in the classroom. That being said, there is high anxiety for many students around fellow students, and this is serving as a detriment in making friends. It is an area that program staff and parents need to develop both inside and outside the program.

Responses

➢ Have our program staff create a handbook of basic games and activities that students can practice at home with parents

➢ Ask parents to participate in one activity near the end of each session

➢ Revisit the Live 5-2-1-0 Playboxes, an initiative with Fraser Health and New Westminster Parks and Recreation. The playboxes were filled with equipment and placed in parks throughout the city to encourage physical activity, but the equipment was all stolen after approximately one month

➢ Promote the different team sports that are offered in New Westminster. We have relationships with Canadian Tire JumpStart Foundation and Kidsport who both offer subsidies for participation

Finding 6

Student leadership is impacting the community

Description

The experiences in the program are creating exceptional student leaders in the program. The oldest students in the program are in Grade Five. Program staff has expectations that Grade Five students act as leaders within the program and set an example for the younger students. Community School Coordinators have regularly observed this since the program's inception in 2013.

Parent and caregiver interviews have provided insight into how these students are also demonstrating leadership outside the program. Some are taking more active roles in supervising young children in their home communities. For example, as one parent pointed out, "She wants to start taking a leadership role for younger students and children around her housing complex. She will herd them around and help take care of them during group gatherings." Another participant's grandparents shared how their son had become more helpful, moving away from a selfish mindset: "He sees other kids try something and he'll help them out now. He wasn't like that before. He just wanted to win all the time." Mirroring these sentiments, another parent points out their daughter is now a "helper… [who] likes to learn a skill and then help younger students understand."

In addition to the older students developing leadership skills, the evidence is showing that students as young as Grade Two are wanting to have an influence on younger students: "He (Grade 2 student) wants to be a leader and set examples for younger students. He has learned compassion, and he can relate to different people." Students told parents that they enjoyed it when the program staff acted as "cheerleaders" for the students and it is an action that many have taken away with them from the program. From the interviews, we have learned that students tend to observe the various leadership types and traits and customize them to fit what they prefer.

Significance

It is special, as part of a Community School, to know that we are playing an integral role in creating young leaders. For instance, Jumpsport students' parents and caregivers reported that their children are experiencing bullying behaviour amongst peers at school. We believe if more students participate in Jumpsport and learn these skills we can continue to assist in eliminating this behaviour. This is important both in school and out of school. Students are learning how to recognize positive behaviours and replicate them around friend groups, peers, siblings, and other younger children. Therefore, the Jumpsport participants' leadership skills are having an impact outside the program.

Responses

➤ Offer training for Community School Coordinators regarding the redesigned curriculum and its core competencies
➤ Educate students regarding the language surrounding core competencies
➤ Provide leadership opportunities for older students in the program

➢ Develop a tool to help students understand and reflect on what they are learning and doing

Finding 7
Students attending Jumpsport are feeling empowered

Description

Empowerment has emerged as a theme for many students in the program. According to parents, students are developing a mindset where they want to take initiative and be their own self-managers. In one case, a student who often has one-on-one assistance in a classroom has made significant strides towards independence from the program. His parent shared, "He feels like a big boy because he walks to the gym by himself after school. He has an after-school snack that is labeled for him to eat before or during the program. He likes this little bit of independence. He feels like a grown up."

The mother who spoke about her child taking a leadership role around their apartment complex added details about the change in how her daughter is taking care of herself. "Before she started taking Jumpsport, she was very reactive. She would sit back and let things happen to her that could have been prevented. Her confidence has led to more proactive actions, especially regarding her feelings." Students from Jumpsport are making tremendous strides in caring about their wellbeing and not always having to rely on others to take the lead.

Significance

Empowering students is vital for developing them into leaders and building their self-esteem. Students in the program do not always receive the positive reinforcement that we, as Community School Coordinators, would like to see. Through the interviews, we learned that students have had difficult upbringings and faced struggles such as absent parents, bullying from peers, and a lack of overall support. Jumpsport is building a belief in students that they are capable of doing things that they may previously have been told they could not do. For younger students attending Jumpsport, it is their responsibility to get from the classroom to the gym and feeling like a "grown-up". Older students are taking control of the actions and decisions that most affect them. A parent said to one coordinator that her child feels most empowered when active.

Responses
- ➤ Community School Coordinators will work more with school staff to identify students in need of extra support
- ➤ Allow students to lead activities or bring ideas to each session

Conclusion and Next Steps

Conclusion

At the beginning of our research, we identified four areas of impact we wanted Jumpsport to have on students. The impacts were the following:
- ➤ Become physically active for life.
- ➤ Become empathetic towards their classmates and teachers.
- ➤ Become strong self-managers with high levels of emotional resiliency.
- ➤ Build healthy relationships with peers and adults.

There were a number of key indicators that lead us to believe that students from the Jumpsport program will strive to be active for life. Most importantly, interviews and surveys showed that students were developing physical skills that they wanted to utilize outside the program in community sports.

A feeling of increased student confidence and empowerment were the main findings that indicated they were becoming stronger self-managers with more resiliency. Numerous parents and caregivers reported their children not waiting for something to happen to them, but rather, taking charge and telling someone if they were upset.

The adults in the program have proven themselves as role models. They have not only bonded with the students but are providing the skills necessary for students to foster other healthy relationships with adults in their respective families and the community.

An impact that we were hoping to see, but students are still struggling with, is building friendships with peers. The program is succeeding in bringing students together and improving teamwork; however, close bonds are not being formed.

What comes next?

This experience has left us incredibly proud of Jumpsport. The program has made tremendous strides over the past couple of years, and we have clear ideas how to continue its success, while still making improvements.

The first step that we, as Community Schools, must take is to develop a clear staff succession plan. In this line of work, we experience high rates of staff turnover. Many of our staff are college students who move on to full-time work once they graduate. We must ensure that incoming staff receive strong training and can lead students effectively. Our relationship with Douglas College will continue to offer high-quality fieldwork student volunteers. The program also provides an opportunity for high school students to get more involved with leadership opportunities, which could lead to employment for them in the future.

We have learned that simply gathering students in a gym and expecting friendships to form is naive on our part. Community School Coordinators will work with program staff to make intentional efforts to teach students friendship building skills. This initiative could include bringing in guest facilitators, provide staff training, and offer more cooperative-based games and activities within the program.

Lastly, Community School Coordinators will continue to collaborate with school staff and community partners to ensure students who would most benefit from the program receive access. Furthermore, we must be capable of offering students ways they can practice their physical and teamwork skills beyond the school setting. We will strive to connect more with youth sports organizations and City of New Westminster Parks and Recreation, so students have that opportunity with no or minimal barriers.

Despite the abundance of valuable data gathered, we are left somewhat surprised at the number of parents who confided in us that they do not ask their child about Jumpsport or how their school day went. This could be a sign of a lack of interest or the societal symptom of time poverty and how working parents do not get to spend as much time with their child. We would like to investigate this issue further to examine how it relates to some of our other intended impacts and findings.

School District 43 (Coquitlam)

Community School After School Programs

Jeff Stromgren, Dasha Belskaya, Tong Guan, Steve Roos,
Laura McKinley, Shreya Qazi

Introduction to the Organization

School District 43 mission is to ensure quality learning opportunities for all students of all ages. Our Community Schools have been organized in places and for people who may not be assured equal access to learning opportunities due to facing vulnerability in one form or another. Our thriving system of community schools and community partnerships focus joint community and school resources on student success. Our community schools offer opportunities that all children deserve and help remove barriers to learning and growing. Intentionally, we are using the governance model of community schools to help children and families stay connected; to peers, to significant adults, school and community.

The community school strategy can have its broadest, deepest, and most sustainable impact when a school system and all its community partners have shared intentionality. A multisite/multi-partnered effort embeds the vision of community schools in the principles and practices, beliefs, and expectations of its schools, partners agencies, families, and community members. As the effort scales up, the community schools vision becomes the new culture. In that new culture, individuals and organizations alike share the work, responsibilities, and benefits of improved results for children, families, schools, and communities.

Before and after school programming expands learning opportunities for children beyond a traditional 9am-3pm school day to create a coherent educational experience. The out-of-school time climate may be less formal but is of good quality and is experiential. Most importantly, programs should focus on the social and emotional development of children. It is through the lens of Social and Emotional Learning (SEL) of children that we undertake the evaluation of the impact our programs are having.

Our after school programs are designed to engage kids in a variety of experiences intended to develop them in ways that reveal significant personal growth; enough that is noticeable to those with a front row seat to their development (i.e., parents, teachers, administrators). Our organization's theory of change identifies our unique position in the community which gives us access children and families, allows us to leverage our resources to recruit others to help, and provide connections for children and families to a wide range of other people, organizations and services in the community.

Evaluation Methodology

The purpose of our evaluation was to determine the type and quality of impact that the Community School After School Programs are having on the population we are serving. To understand this, we explored two broad research questions:

> ➤ What type and quality of impact are we having on our participants?
> ➤ What aspects of our program are causing this impact?

Over the course of the project, we (a) developed and refined our ideas of intended impact and indicators, (b) designed and implemented a mixed methods outcome evaluation using both qualitative and quantitative means to collect and analyze data, (c) identified findings, and (d) considered the implications to those findings for program improvement and innovation.

This project began with a focus on the work of identifying and clarifying the intended impact of the Community School After School Programs. Once the ideas of impact had been developed, we used the Heart Triangle™ model to identify qualitative and quantitative indicators focused on the mental, behavioral and emotional changes in our participants. We then used these indicators to design a qualitative interview protocol and a quantitative questionnaire to measure our progress toward achieving our intended impact.

Qualitative Data Collection and Analysis

For the qualitative portion of the evaluation, we designed an in-depth interview to gain data about the structural, qualitative changes resulting from our program. We used a purposeful stratified sampling technique to select a representative sample from the population we serve. Our population size was 506. Our sample size was 23 and was drawn from the following strata of our population:

> - Parents of children in grades K – 5 attending elementary community schools in School District 43 who have attended multiple after school programs
> - Students in grades 6 – 8 attending middle community schools in School District 43 who participated in multiple after school programs
> - The participants in the quantitative interviews ranged on a broad spectrum of families with economic vulnerabilities

Our interview team consisted of five staff members and a community partner. Interviewers who did not participate in the Project Impact cohort meetings were trained in qualitative data collection and analysis before conducting interviews.

We then conducted one-on-one interviews lasting between 45 minutes and one hour in length with a sample from the identified strata of the population. Interviewers gathered the data by capturing the conversation through written notes during the interviews and filled in the notes immediately after the interview to obtain a substantive rendering of the interview.

We analyzed the data inductively using a modified version of thematic analysis. Interviewers implemented the first three phases of thematic analysis (becoming familiar with the data, generating initial codes and identifying themes) for each interview. The interviewers analyzed the raw data by reviewing each interview four times through each of the four lenses to illuminate a different aspect of what the data revealed about the research question. The data were then distributed into four categories to serve as an initial set of codes. Then, intra-interview themes were generated based on the pervasive insights from the data. This process allowed us to interpret the meaning and significance of the data from each interview.

Next, we pooled the data analyses and initial themes together and implemented the next two phases of thematic analysis (reviewing themes, defining and naming themes). We reviewed the initial themes as a team to identify the overarching and inter-interview themes that emerged from the full scope of our data analysis to illuminate the collective insights and discoveries. We mapped these themes visually and examined them in various ways to gain a greater definition of the features of the themes, causes, and catalysts of the themes, new or surprising insights related to the themes, and relationships between the themes that were revealed in the data. Finally, we determined the most significant and meaningful discoveries and brought them forward as findings to be described in the final phase of thematic analysis, this report.

Quantitative Data and Analysis

For the quantitative portion of the evaluation, we designed a questionnaire to collect data on our quantitative indicators of impact. We administered this instrument to 417 families and had a response of 61. The data were analyzed primarily using measures of central tendency. We identified key insights, patterns, and gaps within the data and incorporated these discoveries into the related findings. The most significant findings from this evaluation are described in the following narrative.

Findings and Response

Finding 1
Connecting the Dots

The first finding from this study was that participants have developed healthy relationships and relationship building skills. Our study reveals that new friendships have been made and that new skills have been learned to help participants relate and connect with one another. Positive changes have occurred in the participants as a result. Parents reported seeing their children grow from being shy and withdrawn to becoming outgoing and confident. They also reported that their children learned to become more open to the perspectives, thoughts, and opinions of others.

Students, and parents of students who participate in our after school programs reveal that relationships are personal in nature, and sustain themselves beyond the program itself into other aspects of their lives. One participant, a middle school student, reported that "most of the friends that I have made are a result of participating in community school programs, and participating has made me appreciate meeting new people and made me more likely to share things that are personal." The notion that "personal" items are being discussed is a strong indicator to our group that the changes are not superficial; rather, that they are the subtle and hard to access feelings that we aim to learn about and improve in our young people. These kinds of personal changes, we believe, will affect their growth and their learning.

In addition to students speaking up about their personal growth, we found examples in our interviews of students who made observations about others in the after school programs. For our team, the opportunity to learn about peer to peer observations would help us understand more deeply how the participants experienced the programs. Reflecting on her relationships with others who had participated, a Middle School aged student said that her own participation "kind of changed the way I saw people…I saw people in a different environment (than school) and saw

35

them grow in confidence. It helped me learn new things about people, that people can be different depending on the situation, like being more outgoing in a program than a class. I learned not to judge someone on how they present." This student's descriptive observations effectively illustrate our intended impact of the participants growing through rich social learning about themselves and understanding of others.

Significance and Response

The quantitative data analysis showed that more than 75% of the respondents reported an increase in new friendships. Additionally, data support our hope that there is a substantial increase in the participant's comfort level in introducing themselves to new children after participating in after school programs within Community Schools.

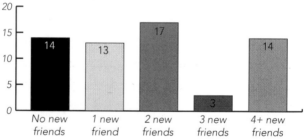

Figure 1. Number of new friendships developed in after school programs reported by participants

For participants in after school programs, there was a noticeable improvement in the ability to develop and maintain positive, healthy connections with their peers. Instinctively we believe that healthy friendships are an important factor influencing the well-being of young people and are critical to developing and strengthening social and emotional skills for lifelong relational success.

Our interviews with participants and parents also offer hints about organizational growth. Teaching our Leaders to pay attention to specific aspects of each child that may require growth can help facilitate the development of relationship building skills. We will now ask leaders to keep these kinds of questions in mind when instructing any type of after school program, "Who is shy? Who lacks confidence? Who is outgoing? Who may need to pay more attention to the needs of others?". By having instructors monitor this kind of behavior more intentionally, we may be able to help foster social connections between kids that helps them work through their specific issues.

Finding 2
They Don't Know What They Don't Know

Perhaps the most surprising finding in our study wasn't what parents knew about their children, rather, it was what they didn't know about our intentions relating to the Social and Emotional Learning (SEL) of their children. We found that we had not been explicit about our intentions. Parents indicated they thought they were showing up to discuss "soccer," "music," or "fencing" as they scratched their heads wondering what we were asking questions about changes in their children's emotions, ability to make friends or the significance of a new adult in their children's lives. When asked about growth, parents answered within the confines of skill development; "my son has gotten way better kicking with his left foot" was more typical than "he really figured out when to back off to let others have a chance."

The most significant indicator that we had been unclear with our intentions was the amount of decoding and explanations about the various elements of our intended impacts. In recognizing that parents were uninformed when it came to our intentions of helping their children achieve SEL outcomes, we also posit that the community at large is also uninformed about the intentions we have. We believe that by helping parents and the greater community understand the social and emotional value of after school programs, we can better engage the community to the benefit of children and families. Thus, we have identified a finding that will help direct our work planning in the future.

The large percentage of "Neither agree or disagree" in our quantitative data has provided insight on another finding that impacts our understanding of what parents are thinking about when it comes to after school programs. In our quantitative data analysis, we recognized that a large number of parents chose "Neither Agree or Disagree," and this made us stop to consider why. As we poured through qualitative interview data, we noticed that parents were repeatedly left a little stumped when it came to answering some of the questions that were aimed at intentions beyond the subject matter of the after school program. Our learning then is that parents do not have the same intentions about the social and emotional effects of after school programs as we do. We also learned that they require extensive "decoding" of the language associated with understating a child's social and emotional self, as after school programs are typically seen as only as a recreation activity.

As a result of the parents and community not being more thoroughly informed on our intentions, we feel that it is a strong possibility that kids also did not go into the programs with an explicit understanding of the Social and Emotional benefits. Making clear the learning intentions will produce the learning outcomes we are trying to achieve more readily adopted by the participants. As an example, one of our intentions is to help children build relationships with new adults, but because of the disconnect between our plans and our stakeholder group's awareness of our intentions, the engagement of our community has not been as strong as we believe it could be.

Significance and Response

Community Engagement will strengthen our attachment to all stakeholders and being explicit about the SEL outcomes will help us achieve our aims. We believe this is a significant finding because conversations with members of the community will result in a multiplying effect. We hope that those who have been engaged will talk more openly to others, they will spend the time that they otherwise may not have to consider the ramifications of the programming and think beyond the program title and subject matter. One parent of a grade 3 girl suggested that she would pay more attention to the kinds of changes she sees in her daughter as a result of making new friends in the after school programs. With parents paying closer attention to this kind of outcome, we will be able to act more communally to help her.

Community Engagement, for our purposes, is illustrated by a series of both formal and informal relationships with individuals, organizations, and agencies of the public to enhance our students' learning and wellbeing outcomes. Community partners include community organizations, individuals, sporting clubs, education and training providers, government organizations, local businesses, and industry. Sharing our intentions through these partnerships provides an opportunity for SD43 community schools to offer a range of experiences, real life learning opportunities, support and resources that may not be available within the school to improve students' learning and well-being outcomes. Making clear our intentions will broaden the opportunities for students in our programs.

SD43 Community Schools must play a critical role in supporting diversity and provide opportunities for other community members to model and foster respectful relationships between learners and all members of the community. To this end, we have established an intervention that we can apply very quickly to help us make clearer our intentions to parents and the community at large. We will begin designing "Advisory Committees" to act as our sounding boards, and to learn information about what our community expects and wants. They will become our conduit to share our intentions more broadly than ever before. As a result of this finding, we are inspired to share the information from the Advisory Committees to the greater population of stakeholders via newsletters, word of mouth, and through structures like our breakfast programs and other places parents, students and the community gather in our schools.

Another potential experiment we could run in the future would be to make explicit in our advertising to parents the SEL intentions. Since parents are still the primary information provider and decision makers around programs the students take, we think it will strengthen our ability to achieve desired outcomes if we can communicate the way each program fosters the SEL outcomes such as "making connections to a significant adult" or "developing empathy for others." This finding would indicate that building SEL language and concepts into our advertising and information posters would make a lot of sense.

Finding 3
Follow the Leader?

When we started our work on the evaluation of after school programs in our Community Schools, we expected that participants would report a sense of connectedness to the adult leader/instructor. While it was clear that parents of younger elementary aged children reported a sense of connectedness with adult leaders/instructors, this was not necessarily the case with our older participants. Middle school participants reported the opportunity to develop strong, healthy peer connections, but there was a noticeable absence of reports about the same strong connection to an adult in the program. They identified that instructors helped create a sense of safety, and some sort of connection to their community, and they believed their instructors cared for them, but interviews did not reveal strong feelings of connection to the leader as a remarkable element of the program.

Our study shows the importance of the Adult Leader to our youngest participants. Children who were found to be both passionate about or indifferent to the program subject matter (i.e., soccer, drama or music) were all found to report on having strong relationships with the program leader. This theme and our learning about the importance of this connection for our youngest participants are scattered throughout many of our findings in this study (see Findings #4 and #6). Much of what we learned in this finding has to do with the lack of connectivity between middle school-aged kids and the leaders of our programs.

One middle school-aged student reported the following about her participation: "I made new friends and found that my comfort level in new situations had improved." She went on to say, "Students in the program made me feel more welcome in the program but not the instructor, even though they were kind." This sentiment illustrates an assumption we made about the importance of the instructor. When we reviewed other participant notes, we didn't see as overt of a statement, but the absence of any kind of praise or excitement about the instructor gave us our understanding. We recognize from the full body of work that the instructor is a critical element. However, we have learned anew that our oldest participants from the middle schools are attending with their own intentions of creating peer connections and largely ignoring the importance of the relationship with the leader or instructor.

Overall, the quantitative data analysis showed us over 75% of the connections with adult staff were warm and positive and 23% were undecided about the connection. The data were collected from both elementary and middle school levels, which leads us to believe the 23% is the noticeable absence of the strong connection with the adult staff which the middle school level participants could have experienced.

Figure 2. Warm and positive connections with adult staff

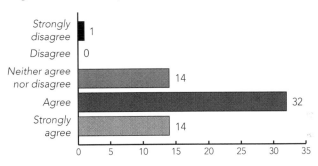

Significance and Response

While middle school-aged participants seemed to appreciate the role their instructors played, they did not report the level of connectedness that we believed they would have experienced. This is a rather significant finding because it impacts the way we as organizers and community developers approach the programming at the middle school level. We might be better off trying to create opportunities for peer to peer relationships with instructors or leaders from a secondary school or college where the relationship between youth can be more fully developed in a way that has been identified here. If the participants saw the "leader" as more of a peer, we may have better luck in developing more meaningful connections.

We have identified multiple factors at play requiring a look deeper into the developmental stage our Middle School participants are at and the importance of peer connectivity to them. We may choose in the future to be more experimental in our efforts to help the connectivity to adults be more prevalent in the older group of participants experiences. We might try different timelines for programming, types of programs, and leaders for those programs that are more in-tune to this age group. Until then, we are happy to have learned that it is not as much a focus for them as it has been for us in the development of the programs. Regardless of what we may learn next, this was an important finding for us and identifies an area to target for improvement. If it is true that the significance that a single caring adult can have in the lives of young people, then we want to find ways of helping those kinds of relationships develop.

Finding 4
Do as I Do

Though our primary intention for after school programs is to help develop participants' social and emotional well-being, it is impossible to ignore the evidence from our impact study that suggests improvement in personal health habits of our participants has increased as the result of good modeling by the instructor. In our study, parents have reported significant health habit benefits being born from good modeling by the instructor. These health habits have been both physical as well as social and emotional in nature.

As is discovered in several of our findings, the role of the instructor is paramount in the children's uptake of these health habits. An example of physical health habits that were modeled for our students was that of drinking water before during and after physical exertion, the value of stretching (even in art programs when you prepare the hand muscles), and the importance of eating a healthy snack to alleviate fatigue. One parent reported her son to have grown into the idea that a healthy snack will stop him from becoming whiny or frustrated. Another discovered that her daughter "...connected the dots between eating a healthy snack after school and working through her desire to take a nap as she did after school last year when she was in Kindergarten."

Social and Emotional Health habits that were modeled by our instructors became part of the way our participants began showing up in other parts of their lives. When introduced as part of the pre-class warm up, "Meditation" became a regular practice of several of our students (even at a very young age). When our instructors utilized breathing techniques that were aimed at calming the body before painting, or at recovery from physical exertion, the children were reported to have used these techniques in other parts of their lives. "My child stops at the Lego table to take deep breaths when the project starts going sideways," reported a father of a grade 3 student.

Significance and Response

The quantitative data analysis revealed over 65% reported positive behaviors were learned from the after school programs, while 30% reported they are undecided.

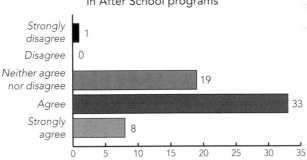

Figure 3. Increased positive behavior learned in After School programs

Children who make early commitments to healthy living are more likely to lead healthy lives. Reminders from all the significant adults in our children's lives can help in establishing beneficial health habits. There is a significant role, then, that the leaders of our programs play in the uptake of healthy habits for our children and as an extension, their family. Our leaders must have in mind that children are monitoring their actions and emulated. It means they should overtly take the time to remind children and model for children the various ways each can do their part in affecting the health habits of children.

The significance of this finding is not limited to the children's learning. Now that we have discovered this idea, the inclusion of this finding makes sense in the way we prepare our leaders, making sure they understand the depth of influence they have on children when it comes to health habits. The findings hold true whether the program leader is teaching Physical Activity, or Lego, or arts. One parent of a middle school student from an after school DJ program noted that the instructor modeled sleeping and getting to bed at an appropriate time. The instructor had mentioned to the class that sleeping plays a significant role in hand stability, so if you want to scratch with skill, they'd better rest up. A mother was so impressed stating that because her son loved the instructor so much in his DJ program that he has been going to bed an hour earlier with the intention of becoming a better DJ.

Finding 5
The New and Improved ME

Through our conversations with parents, it is evident that the programs have an influence on the development of children's self-concept, and that Children who have participated are keen to show off the "New and Improved ME." Parents shared that they have seen their children understand more complicated facets of their self-identity. Children who were once timid, shy, or angry are now developing relationships with adults and peers, controlling their anger, and showing a willingness to try new activities. Students are showcasing their new characteristics such as compassion, empathy, patience, independence, and articulation when faced with new situations involving adults and/or peers.

During their time in after school programs, they are encountering new environments, people, and scenarios and they are pushing the boundaries of what they can do with their abilities. Parents reported a shift in their children's behavior; children now see themselves as the leaders and role models to their peers. In the after school programs, students are provided with an opportunity to complete tasks independently and as a team which allows them to explore and learn about who they are and who they want to be.

In an interview of a mother to a grade four student, she welled up with tears when discussing the skills her daughter has learned through the after school programs. She stated that her daughter "has been given the opportunity to explore her creativity which has excited her, and she now uses story-telling to express herself to her peers and adults." This parent also stated that she has seen her daughter "let go of mom" and is more "independent" and making choices more on her own and not looking to mom as often for the "OK."

Significance and Response

The importance of realizing their potential is beneficial to children at a young age as it will help set them up for success in the future. Children are exploring their creative side which contributes to the way they view themselves and the role that they have in the world. Through participation and interactions with others, this allows children to dream, have bigger aspirations, and believe in themselves. This "new" potential provides a catalyst for new thoughts and higher expectations of oneself. If children see themselves in a new light, with potential and optimism, it can lead to reducing their vulnerability.

The data analysis revealed over 65% of participants experienced the development of self-confidence, 44% reported increased compassion towards others, and 57% reported increased social awareness since participating in after school programs.

see chart on next page

From this point forward in our program planning, it makes sense to us to try to showcase the New and Improved ME whenever possible. Giving the kids a chance to show everyone their strengths, high energy and enjoyment

Figure 4. Increased self-confidence

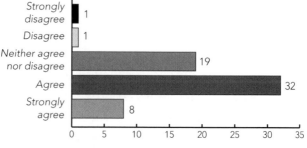

Figure 5. Increased social awareness

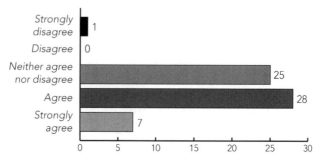

will play a role in spreading the message to our community about what we are trying to help kids accomplish.

Finding 6
Who am I showing up for?

Within our impact study we isolated a finding of why participants are choosing to attend the program's opportunities; was it based on their personal interest level of developing new skills? Or was it for the social aspect of relationships within the program? Our results show that participants are choosing to increase the number of programs they participate in because of the meaningful relationships they have created within the programs. This finding is important as it identifies the spark for the attendance of programs, which leads to the intended development of participants within the community programs.

Through our interviews and quantitative data collection, we discovered the importance of understanding why participants were attending programs. Parents told us that initially, they register their children within the program for three reasons – the child is interested in the content of the program, or the child knows that they will create new connections within the program, or the impact that leader has on the child is the driving force for initial attendance. The data show that after the initial registration the participants continue to be motivated to attend the programs because of the connection with the leader. One parent of a girl in grade 2 reported, "My daughter was feeling sick and did not attend school, however, was adamant that she will attend the after school program because of her connection to the program leader." This testimony directly displays the importance of a caring adult that can make healthy connections with all participants, and those connections are the fire that continuously sparks the motivation to attend programs.

The type of relationships being built between participants and leaders are proving to be a strong factor in improving consistency in attendance and increased willingness to do more programs. In an interview response about what her son would consider when selecting a program to attend, one mother of an elementary aged boy said that her son "...didn't want to attend programs where the leaders were mean, and that was the reason he was not registered for the program where his interest level was high." The boy liked the content but chose not to go to the program because he did not like the leader. This points to a potential deterrent to attending programs.

Significance and Response

The consistent trend in parent answers to why students were taking programs points to our belief that when the child builds a meaningful relationship with the leader the child starts to feel as though they are valued. This, in turn, leads to the motivation to attend regularly. The quantitative data analysis reveals an overwhelming majority of children that participated in the after school programs have a positive experience. Additionally, the data showed that 100% of the participants who participated previously in after school programs would participate again (see appendix for data).

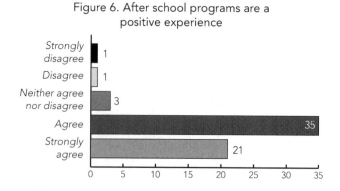

Figure 6. After school programs are a positive experience

When we hear responses like this one from a mother of two kids in one of our community schools, we start to see that the kids will, in fact, make decisions based on who is in the program when it comes to a leader. This mother shared, "My kids signed up for that program because they heard consistent laughter coming from there after school and they wanted to be part of that." The creation of the environment by the leader cannot be understated as it contributes to the perception the community has about the programs and it motivates others to join. Additionally, it is important to note one parent stated, "My children attend the same program with the same leader for years due even though the content does not change because of their connection with the leader."

That kids are showing up to programs due to the leaders' qualities is an amazing finding for us because it helps us make decisions about who to involve and what we might evaluate regarding qualities that kids like about instructors. Now that we know the instructor plays such a critical role in their decision making, we can learn what exactly they like; qualities, personality types, and other things that kids may be able to tell us about the leaders. With this info we can adjust programs, leader development strategies, and recruitment efforts. These adjustments can help our community schools to assist with the personal development of participants.

Finding 7
Building Skills Builds Self-Esteem

As we are planning the slate of after school programs, we often try to include options for families from sports, music, the arts, life skills, and academic support. The intention of course in each program is twofold; skill building and then the social and emotional development which provides the strongest impetus for our team. In this study, we have found that students who build skills, also develop a more profound sense of self-esteem. The acquisition of skills in any of the disciplines offers a sense of accomplishment, attachment, and becomes a source of pride for the participant. From our interviews, we feel like the increased skill development has reduced anxiety to participate and increased Self-Esteem.

Children whose parents reported the acquisition of new skill also referred to higher levels of self-esteem. A grade 2 girl who participated in multiple Fencing programs developed incredible self-confidence, not just in the sport but on the playground as well. Her mother spoke of how she was out recruiting other kids to come to Fencing because "I want to show them how good I have become." This seems a bit like bragging, but the mother reported that the girl had been very isolated at breaktimes in school (lunch and recess) and feared going up to other kids. Before developing the skills in Fencing, she was not able to start these kinds of conversation that might result in asking the other kids to play or to join her in her play.

Further reports of this kind of behaviour came from the father of a grade 1 boy whose prowess in "Music Adventure" had resulted in increased "Showing off at family gatherings where he set up drums to show his skills." Prior to deepening his skill set in music creation, the boy tended to shy behind mom's or dad's legs when other adult family members came to the house and didn't want mom to leave when dropping off at school. The quantitative data support our position on the decreasing levels of anxiety about school.

see chart on next page

Figure 7. Decreased anxiety about school

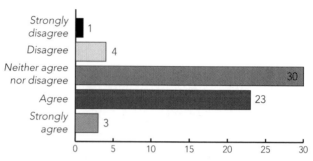

Significance and Response

The significance of such a finding is that we can see the link between programs and the outcomes we are trying to impact. The development of social skills is as essential to our Community Development Facilitators who coordinate the programs as the physical skill obtained. But the link between the two has been illuminated by this project. If we can make sure that kids are connecting to programs that capture their imaginations and link to their passions, and they learn new skills in those projects, then we should begin to see a steady rise in their self-esteem and connectivity to other kids and adults as a result.

Also significant is the notion that the skills built in school carry over to the classroom and reflect academic success. In recognizing that parents often didn't differentiate between after school programs and classroom or in-school experiences, we can work to link student success in after school programs to success in school as it is communicated to parents. Allowing teachers then to access the insights of the instructors in the future, may yield useful information to share with parents about the successes in school as a whole; thus, tying the value of after school programs to the success of the participant in school.

Conclusion and Next Steps

Our findings give us strong insights into how well programming has achieved the aims we had intended giving us proof of good work but also showing us ways to improve. The study has proven to us that students are growing socially and emotionally while having fun and learning some life skills. It has also given us insight into areas we can improve our programs to better achieve our intended results. The team of Community Development Facilitators, program providers, school administrators, and District Coordinators can use this information to inform our decision making around what kinds of programs to focus on, to help develop our program instructors and advise our partners of positive steps forward in their development and growth.

We believe that our theory of change is strong; that we have a unique ability to serve children and families through the provision of affordable programs that are run after school in the school itself. Our unique position in the community gives us access to public facilities, proximity to children and families, and a central location in neighbourhoods that have historically been inhabited by our most vulnerable citizens. Our work is housed within a large public domain, the education system, which also grants us access to knowledge and research that can inform our decision making. Responses to our findings will make their way to the program level and improve further our ability to affect the lives of children and families positively.

We are encouraged that many of the Social and Emotional Learning intentions we hoped to achieve are being accomplished. That is, children are making new friends, building relationships and getting connected. With this in mind, we will continue to encourage leaders and program providers to help foster friendships, teach relationship building skills, and be aware of issues arising from conflict by providing more explicit information to parents and leaders of our programs about the intentions we have for social and emotional learning in our programs we hope to gain stronger support for the programs we run. We look forward to the creation of Advisory Committees in whatever form it may take in each of our community school contexts.

Some surprising elements that we discovered in this process are that we must give deeper thought about how to foster relationships between middle school participants and significant adults, that parents don't see the effects of after school programs on their children much differently than they view "regular school stuff", and that kids will likely choose a program based more on who is there than what the content looks like. Our next steps in the development of after school programs will be aimed at incorporating what we have learned, and about sharing what we have learned with our partners and stakeholders. We believe this will further increase the value of the programs to participants, their parents, and to the schools at large.

Sunshine Coast
Family of Community Schools

Community Schools Programs

Stephanie Anderson, Ted Chisholm, Kirsten Deasey, Wendy Pearson

Organization and Program Overview

The Sunshine Coast Family of Community Schools exists to support vulnerable children and youth across the Sunshine Coast. This is done by strengthening individuals, families, and communities by providing quality programs, lifelong learning opportunities and connections to school and community resources. Each Community School Association works to respond to specific regional challenges, recognizing that each neighbourhood has its own unique identity and needs.

We focused our data collection on children who live in Sechelt or Halfmoon Bay and were in grade 6, 7 or 8. Analysis of 16 in-depth interviews and 79 surveys revealed high levels of success in these intended impact areas.

The Sunshine Coast Family of Community Schools provides programs and support to the entire Sunshine Coast from Langdale to Pender Harbour. We are made up of five individual Associations that work together to service the needs of vulnerable children and build strong and resilient communities in our schools. Our Associations and Community School Coordinators service nine elementary schools and three secondary schools. Two of our Community School Associations, Sechelt and Halfmoon Bay/Chatelech, took part in Project Impact.

Description of Programs

Sechelt and Halfmoon Bay/Chatelech Community School Associations offer programs for students in Kindergarten to grade 12. For the purpose of Project Impact, we chose to focus our lens on students in grades 6-8. The programs we specifically looked at were the Sechelt Youth Centre and Halfmoon Bay's Homework Club, Tween Night and Student Council. The Youth Centre and Tween Night are drop-in programs whereas Homework Club and Student Council are pre-registered.

Intended Impacts

The purpose of this report is to explore the impact that Community School programs have had on two of our communities: Sechelt and Halfmoon Bay. We set out to measure the impact on students who use Community School programs by identifying changes in their habits, attitudes, and beliefs as a result of their participation. To do this, we developed four intended impacts that we hope to achieve:

As a result of Community Schools, children, youth and families:
➤ Feel safe, cared for and connected.
➤ Recognize the importance of creative expression.
➤ Be more self-aware, resilient and confident.
➤ Have a passion for reading.

Evaluation Methodology

The aim of our evaluation was to see what kind and quality of impact the Youth Centre, Homework Club, Tween Night and Student Council programs are having in the population we are serving. To understand this, we explored two broad research questions:
➤ What kind and quality of impact are we having on our recipients?
➤ What aspects of our program are causing this impact?

Over the course of the project, we (a) developed and refined our ideas of intended impact and indicators, (b) designed and implemented a mixed methods outcome evaluation using both qualitative and quantitative means to collect and analyze data, (c) identified findings and (d) considered the implications to those findings for program improvement and innovation.

This project began with a focus on the work of identifying and clarifying the intended impact of programming for participants grades 6-8. Once the ideas of impact had been developed, we used the Heart Triangle™ model to identify qualitative and quantitative indicators of impact focused on the mental, behavioural and emotional changes in our beneficiaries that indicate we are achieving our impact. We then used these indicators to design a qualitative interview protocol and a quantitative questionnaire to measure our progress toward achieving our intended impact.

Qualitative Data Collection and Analysis

For the qualitative portion of the evaluation, we designed an in-depth interview protocol to gain data about the structural, qualitative changes resulting from our program. We used a purposeful stratified sampling technique to select a representative sample from the population we serve. Our population size was 79 children in grades 6-8. Our sample size was 16, and we drew our sample from the following strata of our population:

- ➢ Sechelt and Halfmoon Bay residents
- ➢ Grades 6-8
- ➢ Level of program attendance
- ➢ Registered and Drop-in programs

Our interview team consisted of 3 Community School Coordinators.
We then organized one-on-one interviews lasting from between 45 minutes and one hour in length with a sample from the identified strata of the population. Interviewers gathered the data by capturing the conversation through written notes during the interviews and filled in the notes immediately after the interview to obtain a substantive rendering of the interview.

We analyzed the data inductively using a modified version of thematic analysis. Interviewers implemented the first three phases of thematic analysis (becoming familiar with the data, generating initial codes and identifying themes) for each interview. The interviewers analyzed the raw data by reviewing each interview four times through each of four lenses to illuminate a different aspect of what the data reveal about the research question. The data were then gathered into four categories to serve as an initial set of codes. Then, intra-interview themes were generated based on the pervasive insights from the data. This process allowed us to interpret the meaning and significance of the data from each interview.

Next, we brought all of the data analyses and initial themes together and implemented the next two phases of thematic analysis (reviewing themes, defining and naming themes). We reviewed the initial themes as a team to identify the overarching and inter-interview themes that emerged from the full scope of our data analysis to illuminate the collective insights and discoveries. We mapped these themes visually and examined them in various ways to gain a greater definition of the features of the themes, causes, and catalysts of the themes, new or surprising insights related to the themes, and relationships between the themes that were revealed in the data. We then determined the most significant and meaningful discoveries and brought them forward as findings to be described in the final phase of thematic analysis, this report.

Quantitative Data and Analysis

For the quantitative portion of the evaluation, we designed a questionnaire to collect data on our quantitative indicators of impact. We administered this instrument to 100 and had a response of 79, a 79% response rate. The data were analyzed primarily using measures of central tendency. We identified key insights, patterns, and gaps within the data and incorporated these discoveries into the related findings.

Findings

Finding 1
Hear Me Roar!

Description

Many participants interviewed spoke about how they feel safe in Community Schools. These participants felt confident being themselves, so they were able to "find their voice" by feeling comfortable to speak up for their beliefs, wants and needs. A common theme in the interviews was the feeling of safety the children and youth experience while participating in Community School programs. As part of our qualitative surveys, we asked participants to tell us about what helps them feel safe in our programs. One grade 6 student responded, "I feel accepted in the community because everyone knows who I am." A major theme in the interviews emerged about being known by people involved in their programs. This made participants feel more confident to speak genuinely since the other participants and adults took the time to get to know them.

Another theme we saw emerge was the participants' confidence in their ability to ask for help and problem solve. Many participants responded to questions about conflict by saying that it is not acceptable to do nothing. Many of them acknowledged that making mistakes is not a bad thing but a way to get help and learn something new. As a part of an interview, a grade 6 student talked about what happens when she makes a mistake. She explained, "Instead of keeping it to myself I can ask for help. Instead of asking for the answer, I like to be helped through the solution."

An interesting finding from our quantitative data shows that while many respondents think it is okay to make mistakes, they are having difficulty letting go of them. Figure 1 shows the gap between survey respondents' comfort with making mistakes compared to letting go of them.

see chart on next page

Figure 1. Dealing with Mistakes

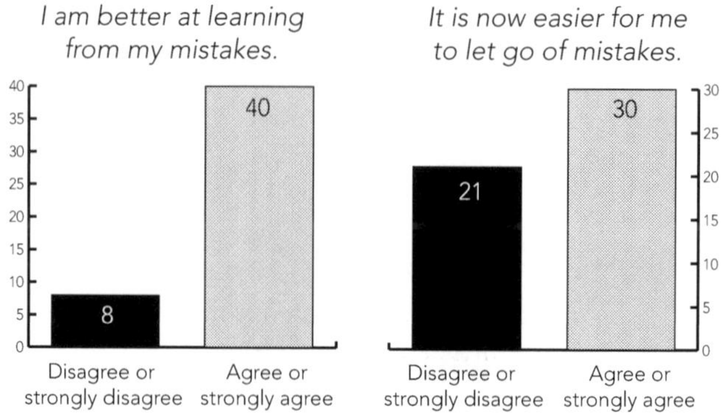

The figure above shows that many participants understood that mistakes could be learned from but a much higher percent reported it is difficult to let the mistakes go. This is interesting because the participants understand that mistakes happen and that they are a part of learning but letting them go remains challenging.

Significance

It is evident from discussions with participants that most feel safe and confident in their schools. Some of these feelings of security come from having caring adults present and involved in their daily lives. Being known in their community was a significant contributor as well. The participants did not see adults as people to solve their problems, but people to act as a guide through difficult situations. This is significant because relationship building is one of the cornerstones of community schools. Their presence and guidance made participants feel that what they had to say was valued and encouraged.

This finding highlighted an area where community schools are very successful. However, one interesting aspect of our data shows that participants are having a harder time letting go of their mistakes than they are accepting it is ok to make them in the first place. These data tell us that we need to work on developing a growth mindset in our schools and programs. Cognitively, the participants are learning from their mistakes, but emotionally they are having difficulty letting go.

Responses

➤ Coordinator, staff and volunteer training in strategies to build stronger relationships with the participants

➤ Provide opportunities for participants to share their knowledge and experiences, and learn to speak on their own behalf with less coaching

➤ Implement growth mindset language and ideas in programs

➤ Role model and discuss mistakes and taking risks in programs

➤ Create a social contract or agreement with participants to encourage asking questions and risks taking.

Finding 2

There's No Place Like Home

Description

As a result of Community Schools, children who were interviewed said that they have an increased feeling of safety to be who they are and express themselves. They realized that it is ok to make mistakes: Instead of feeling embarrassment, they see mistakes as a building block to future success. One girl we interviewed talked about her feelings about taking risks and how her thoughts have changed through the support that she receives at our programs. She explained, "It makes me feel ok about not being perfect."

Through the support of safe adults and strong peer support, many interviewed seem to have been given a sense of soothing and reassurance that others can be depended upon for support and encouragement. One grade 6 girl we interviewed commented, "What makes me feel safe is feeling comfortable, it's nice that there are people there to support me when I need it."

Many interviewed felt more confident acting independently and making their own free choices. By providing a safe space, they were able to build connections and find other children who are like-minded. Through developing these connections and friendships, the participants interviewed displayed increased self-confidence. Children said, "I am not judged," which is a catalyst for feeling safe, and when they feel safe they give themselves the freedom to indeed be themselves.

Our quantitative data confirm this finding as well. The figure below highlights responses to the survey statement, "I am more comfortable asking questions when I am unsure of something." Only 10% of respondents disagreed or strongly disagreed with this statement. Figure 2 shows the level of comfort respondents feel when asking questions in a program.

Figure 2. Comfort with Asking Questions

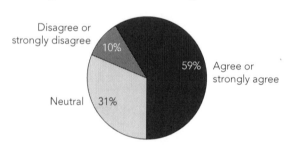

This figure shows that the majority of participants feel safe in their environments and can take risks by asking questions. Speaking up and asking for clarification can be difficult for children who struggle anxiety.

Significance

Community School programming provides a safe space for children to express themselves, giving them an increased sense of belonging and social acceptance. Programs are located in participants' communities, and the accepting and supportive relationships with peers and adults provides them with the confidence to be themselves. Our programming provides our participants with more than just a place to be; our programs give them the confidence to express who they really are. We need to continue to support our participants and give them continued access to safe space. We will continue to support participants' successes and confidence by offering a safe place for exploring themselves and develop relationships with other children and adults. This finding illuminates the social and emotional needs of our participants, shows us how important supportive peers and adults are in their development, and reinforces the positive influence of the supportive community that we provide.

Responses

➢ Staff development, focusing on communication, philosophy, and behaviour
➢ Invite community members into the programs (familiar faces)
➢ Invite older student mentors and role models
➢ Increase parent involvement
➢ Create a more welcoming and student-owned space
➢ Promotions and letters home so everyone is receiving the same message
➢ Identify participants who are feeling unsafe and get their input

Finding 3

One is the Loneliest Number

Description

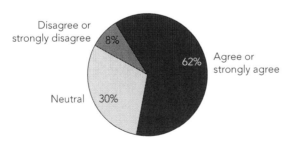

Figure 3. Exploring New Ideas

Participants who reported social anxiety and difficulty with making friends reported feeling accepted, able to be themselves, and more confident moving forward, with some participants using that confidence to engage in other programs in the community, and to start a Genders & Sexuality Alliance (GSA) at their school. In our interviews, participants reported being interested in getting involved in social justice issues, or in being a child and youth worker "which I never would have thought of before." As one youth put it in an interview, "Seeing everyone else being confident, not happy, but being who they are is inspiring, heartwarming. I can do that as well, be confident as well."

Significance

It is important to continue to provide spaces where children and youth have a chance to mix. Although there are opportunities to do this, they are usually fairly structured activities like sports, art, musical theatre, school leadership initiatives, and recreation classes, where children and youth are focused on 'doing' and participating with adult guidance and direction. We found that youth of this age group connected more with receiving a safe space to be themselves more than learning a new skill.

Many participants are exploring LBGTQ2 ideas within their peer groups. A surprise finding is our programs are giving them a safe, inclusive space to provide an open forum and opportunity to discuss gender and sexuality issues. Community Schools have traditionally provided structured programs. However, our data speak to the importance of providing unstructured and inclusive programs such as lounges and youth centres. Within these unstructured spaces, there are safe adults and inclusive language, supporting youth to feel comfortable exploring different social topics. Moving forward, it is important to recognize that successful programming does not always involve 'doing' something. More emphasis must be placed on creating strong peer-to-peer and peer-to-adult relationships, and build opportunities for students to explore their own interests and issues within supportive environments.

Responses

➢ Create space and time for unstructured peer interaction time
➢ Implement 'Circles' on diversity topics
➢ Institute interviews on a regular basis
➢ Invite guest speakers to talk about diversity topics

➢ Replicate meaningful conversations in classrooms

➢ Develop new types of communication with schools

➢ Promote awareness through supporting things such as Mental Health week, etc.

➢ Adopt these ideas into organizational vision

➢ Create programs that draw youth from multiple neighbourhoods

Finding 4

The Secret Ingredient is Passion

Description

Many participants we interviewed had a lot to say about their confidence, relationships, and values. What we did not see was the relationship between Community School programs and developing new passions. When we asked interviewees about their passions, we were met with blank looks on their faces. Some participants responded that they were passionate about reading and exploring new topics through books. One participant was asked about what they are passionate and responded, "I'm more passionate about reading. [Afterschool programs] have inspired me to read more." Seeing a passion about reading was positive. However, this is where passion stopped.

When asked about other passions that had come out of Community School programs we received many answers like, "I like…" and "I enjoy…" but nothing about "I love…" or "I can't wait to…." When we asked a student about what passion he had that came through Community School programs he responded by saying. "I learned I was good at dodgeball." This response, while it was nice to hear he was enjoying this activity, did not go beyond the surface of enjoyment.

Although having a passion for topics was not one of our intended impacts, it was an important theme we were looking for in our findings. We found that Community School programs are having high success with social-emotional learning and development. Our use of unstructured programming contributes to this success. However, we want participants to be able to use Community School programs as a forum to have a new experience that lead to new passions. This finding has highlighted an area in which we need to improve.

Significance

Participants were able to connect community schools with their interest in school, discovering new things, gaining self-confidence and making new friends but there was a distinct lack of passion for new activities and subjects. We were hoping to see more passions emerge from these interviews but these types of responses were absent. One of the main purposes of in school and afterschool community programs is to foster and develop new passions.

This highlights an area of improvement for in-school and afterschool programming. As the BC School Curriculum moves into Inquiry-Based Learning, community schools must also follow suit. Inquiry-Based Learning emphasizes a student-initiated, hands-on and self-directed learning model where students are given time and space to develop new areas of interests and passions. Our programming must also move our focus to this approach by using the same model and language to keep the message consistent. We need to be able to take areas of interest to areas of passions by introducing new topics and supporting their growth through programs and resources. Moving forward, we need to try new programs or enhance our existing programs to offer more space for exploration and development of passions.

Responses

> Pull in community 'magnets' (people who are passionate about things)
> Encourage staff and volunteers to showcase things they love to do
> Discovery sessions, introduce new topics and have resources to support them
> Take them new places for new experiences

➢ Partner with local programs to have combined programming (open-ended)

➢ How do you create inquiry-based programs/opportunities?

Finding 5

A Good Book is a Gift you can Open Again and Again

Description

Community School programs on the Sunshine Coast fit a wide variety of niches and perform many different functions. Programs include breakfast and snack programs, school leadership, social-emotional learning programs, after school homework support, licensed after school care programs, as well as after school and evening drop-in programs.

A common thread throughout all of these various programs is literacy and reading. Every single Community School program does its best to include a literacy component. We found from our interviews and qualitative surveys that there is a passion for reading among participants. One student eloquently said during their interview, "I love it when you feel like you are in the moment of a book and get lost in it. It relaxes me and takes me to another world." Not one of our interviewees stated that they hated reading, which reinforced the importance of reading for enjoyment in the program. The responses ranged from, 'I understand that it is important' to 'I love it.' The majority of respondents said they were passionate about it.

On top of having a passion for reading, some respondents found that reading helped them self-regulate. Some expressed that it was relaxing, had a calming effect or helped them sleep. One student stated, "Reading calms me down, I do it before I go to sleep every night. Even if I go to bed late, I still make time to read, and it makes me sleep better." Our most positive feedback on the quantitative survey was in response to, "I am currently reading a book I am excited about." Over 63% either agreed or strongly agreed with this statement. Figure 4 highlights the importance of reading in the respondent's lives.

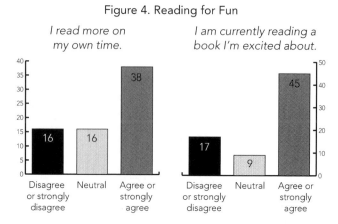

Figure 4. Reading for Fun

Figure 4 shows that most respondents hold reading in high esteem. However, we found the decline in positive responses interesting between the two statements. Fewer participants indicated that they read more on their own time. This may be because they are reading books they are passionate about within Community School programs and do not have time after their long days at school and afterschool activities.

Significance

The value and commitment to literacy and reading in Community School programs appears to be paying off. By making time for reading, it seems many participants have found it enjoyable and relaxing. The gap highlighted in Figure 4 is interesting because although we can see the passion for reading in our programs, some respondents are not carrying this home. Our programs could be doing a better job of encouraging reading at home instead of just in our programs. We recognize that many children in this age group are inundated with afterschool clubs, sports, and activities; leaving them little time to pursue interests on their own once they get home. However, to create lifelong readers Community Schools can be helping them recognize the importance of making time to read during their leisure time.

Responses

➤ Partner with the local library or school librarian to get more books to the participants

- ➢ Create family reading/book club groups within schools
- ➢ Create a Reading on your Own Time program with new books provided
- ➢ Start student lead book clubs at lunchtime
- ➢ Work with the WonderWheels book mobile to get books to students at school
- ➢ Work a reading component into programs
- ➢ Bring in volunteer readers
- ➢ Have local authors make guest visits

Finding 6

Variety is the Spice of Life

Description

Many of the areas Community Schools support are considered small, rural communities. As a result, there is a belief that Community Schools can be limiting, too small or not diverse enough for our participants. Some people may believe we are stuck in our ways with no new ideas or people flowing through our communities. While being a small community can be limiting at times, the children we surveyed were appreciative of our diverse programming and the social variety that it provided. They appreciated their exposure to children from other age groups. Our programs bring children from different classes together and in many cases different geographic regions together. They create new friendships that may not be possible if they were not involved in our programs. Our programs also bring children together who have similar interests.

In these programs, children experience different activities and places, such as taking a trip to the local library, and participants are given experiences they may not have otherwise had in different parts of the community. Community schools can expose participants to new places, experiences, and people.

Through our interviews, we also found that several of our participants are exploring their identity. Our programs provide more diverse social grouping where students can find others that are accepting and supportive. Children and youth connect with others who may have similar questions or problems. This social acceptance provides a safe forum and gives them the confidence to be their true selves. Through exposure to different people one interviewee reflected, I know "more people have anxiety so more people can understand me. It's easier to share my emotions rather than be how people want me to be."

It is important to note that through Community Schools we support safety, acceptance, belonging and empowering children. This is especially important in small rural communities where a lack of diversity can be challenging for participants. The ability of community schools to provide participants with opportunities to meet new people, engage in new activities and explore new ideas was highly valued by participants.

Significance

Sunshine Coast Community Schools provides a forum for new peer groupings, which we found are important in supporting participants. Rather than participating in the same activities with the same children all the time, Community School programming introduced students to new people, ideas and activities. Our participants valued the diversity of our programs much more than we had considered, given the rural nature of our region it is easy for them to stay within the same circles year after year. Moving forward we may look to create more opportunities for programs from different geographical areas to come together. Although this may be challenging given how spread out our schools are, we see tremendous value in bringing groups of students together that would not usually get a chance to know each other.

Responses
- ➤ Bring different groups of children together (from different areas)
- ➤ Bring programs to new and different places
- ➤ Transition events (grade 7)

- ➢ Buddy them up with
- ➢ Regional events such as dances, movie nights, programs (less structured ways)

Finding 7

I Want to Make a Difference

Description

The participants we interviewed showed a very keen interest in being involved with groups and events in their schools. Many of the participants we interviewed participated in multiple groups and activities within their school communities. Many of these participants were intrinsically motivated to help and participate in school and group initiatives. They had a strong desire to be involved and contribute.

Many of the interviews did not delve deeper into their internal motivations about why they participate in different activities, but some students spoke about why they chose to get involved during their own time. During an interview one child said, "I've learned that I can make a difference in our school and make it a better place. My ideas can be used to fundraise or increase the spirit of our school."

It was interesting to see participants connecting the dots between their personal involvement and having an impact on their school. Some spoke of the "Buddy Bench" at Halfmoon Bay Elementary that is a bench where any student can sit if they are feeling lonely or left out and someone will always come to sit with them. One participant explained they "had never seen [a buddy bench] before I came to this school last year and how it helps kids. You can see it really working and sometimes just a good place to hang out." Many understood that through being involved and coming up with fresh ideas they can have a positive impact on their greater community.

The idea that students want to make a difference was a very significant finding because it helps us understand why the participants are involved in many Community School programs. Not one interviewee spoke of being forced by an adult to attend, which showed they are participating because of their own internal motivation.

Significance

Community School programs offer participants a forum to be involved and give back to their community. Students who show up to their school and leave right as the last bell rings might not feel as connected to their school, and thus empowered to impact their school culture. With this information, it is important that Community Schools spend more time empowering students by giving them opportunities to give back to their school or to help other students in need.

It is worth diving deeper into the internal motivations behind why many participants felt it was important to give back. The interviews just began to scratch the surface of why students felt compelled to work and make a difference in their community. Fostering this care for other students and other community members is central to the purpose of Community Schools. Encouraging this behaviour will help create well-rounded children who gain confidence and satisfaction by giving back or helping someone else in need.

Responses
- Work with teachers to include "giving back" into the class time
- Offer more opportunities for student voice and action
- Work with community partners to empower students, such as WE Day
- Start a coast-wide student empowerment group
- Work with students to become school/community leaders
- Connect younger leaders (children) with older leaders (teenagers) and have them work together

Conclusion and Next Steps

Conclusion

Community Schools on the Sunshine Coast provide essential supports for children and youth in our community. Engaging in this process of evaluation helped us understand the impact that we have and the role we play in our community. Through participating in this process, we have also been provided with insight into steps we can take to improve our programs and services.

Next Steps

A focus on implementing strategies to build connections

Participants felt empowered to be themselves and 'find their voice' when they felt known and accepted by the adults and peers in our programs. Moving forward, we will focus on training staff in strategies that will help participants build strong relationships with the adults and the peers in the programs. Staff will be buddied up with participants and encouraged to get to know participants on a deeper level. Staff will also be encouraged to use strategies to help foster closer connections between the children and youth.

Training on 'Growth Mindset'

Staff will also be trained in the importance of using growth mindset language in the programs. Our data indicate that participants viewed mistakes as opportunities to learn and grow. Cognitively, participants understood that mistakes could be powerful in the learning process. However, the children and youth revealed that making mistakes often have a negative emotional impact. Moving forward, we will highlight the acceptance of making mistakes, and we will encourage participants and staff to use a growth mindset language and philosophy.

Creating Centrally located Safe Spaces

The importance of providing central spaces that draw youth from surrounding neighbourhoods emerged as a priority. These programs allow students to move from our rather small, rural communities into spaces where they can meet other like-minded peers. It is essential that these spaces have programming that is open and flexible, and that we allow the issues important to the participants to be the focus. These spaces are also most effective when they are inclusive and safe for all students and can provide a forum for the complex issues which participants at this age are exploring. Staff will be trained in strategies to create safe spaces, build connections between participants, and allow the voices of the participants to be heard.

Building on Student Interests

In order to connect students to new interests and passions, our programming must include opportunities for students to be exposed to new activities and opportunities. A variety of arts and sports opportunities should be offered to participants through our programming. Staff must also be trained to encourage new interests, and support participants to self-reflect and learn about themselves and their passions. As students build interests, staff will be taught strategies to encourage and resource these growing passions.

Connecting Participants with Books to Read & Enjoy

Community school programs will continue to encourage reading, and staff will be taught strategies to connect participants to books they will enjoy. We will look for ways to resource students with a wide variety of books and will build connections with our public libraries and local WonderWheels Bookmobile. We will also encourage students to read as a form of leisure time and will send books home with students to read at home.

Burnaby School District (SD 41)

Connect Workers

Sherri Brattson, Charmaine Calbick, Peter Dubinsky, Colene Friedrich,
Kristen Hellmich, Kevin Herd, Lana Horton, Phillippa McLoughlin

Overview of the Organization and Program

Quality public education has been a community expectation since the first meeting of the Burnaby School Board in 1906. The legacy of quality education and lifelong learning in Burnaby, which began with the amalgamation of early one-room schoolhouses, continues today in 41 elementary schools and 8 secondary schools.

The district enrolls 24,000 students (K-12) and employs 4,000 dedicated employees who are committed to providing all students with a wide variety of innovative, high-quality programs to ensure student achievement in areas that include academics, athletics, trades training, visual and performing arts, social responsibility, and leadership. The District also provides lifelong learning opportunities to more than 16,000 adult learners through an established Community and Continuing Education program.

Our schools reflect the increasingly global nature of the Burnaby community with 4,000 students enrolled in English Language Learning programs. A recent survey of languages spoken in Burnaby homes indicates that more than 100 languages (other than English) are spoken in the homes of Burnaby students. Such diversity has brought rich cultural benefits to Burnaby's communities and schools. The district continues to promote the ideals of multi-culturalism through its policies and school-based initiatives which support cultural respect and understanding.

We're proud of our vibrant neighborhood schools, diverse programs and services and most importantly student achievement. Whether you are a parent with a child in the district, a district employee, a community member or partner, or one of our district students, we invite you to take some time to learn what makes Burnaby unique with its numerous learning opportunities.

Description of Program

In the Burnaby School District, our mandate around activities in the out-of-school time hours is to provide universal, targeted, high-quality programs that meet the diverse needs of our students, with a specific focus on students with higher vulnerability.

The Connect Worker model in the Burnaby School District focuses on supporting vulnerable children and youth through programming and intervention during the critical hours from 3:00 to 6:00 pm. Their effectiveness lies in their ability to create, develop, and sustain caring and strong relationships with all stakeholders. With multiple service providers active at each school site, the Connect Worker builds trusting relationships and utilizes effective communication to ensure all programs run smoothly and attain a high level of quality. They bridge the gap between the classroom and the Out-of-School Time (OST) program providers, by communicating with parents, teachers, and school staff. They also relay information between the school and the OST program regarding students' individual needs, school culture and climate.

Intended Impact

> Schools and community service providers collaboratively deliver quality OST programs tailored to the unique developmental needs of students

> Vulnerable children and youth in quality OST programs develop strong social awareness

➤ Children and youth form meaningful relationships with caring adults in OST programs

Evaluation Methodology

The purpose of our evaluation was to explore the impact of the Connect Worker Model on the quality of out-of-school time programs offered in schools. This evaluation process began with a focus on identifying and clarifying the intended impact of the Connect Worker Model. Once the intended impacts were clarified, and the indicators were identified, we designed an interview protocol to collect qualitative data from a representative sample of OST program partners, managers, and providers. We also developed a questionnaire to track qualitative measures for an inclusive view of our results. The data that was collected from OST program partners about the impact of the Connect Worker Model on the quality of OST programming were analyzed, and themes were identified and translated into findings.

Qualitative Data and Analysis
Our qualitative approach followed the steps below:

Protocol Design
We designed an in-depth interview using the *Heart Triangle* method of question construction. This produced a protocol consisting of 10 questions. The questionnaire was our guide to collect data about the Connect Worker Model from Out-of-School Time (OST) service providers working directly with Connect Workers to deliver OST programs in our schools to children and youth during the critical hours from 3:00 to 6:00 pm. Consideration was given to the environment in which the interview was conducted to ensure a warm, welcoming atmosphere.

Sample
We identified a sample of OST partners, managers, and service providers as a representation of the population of OST providers who work directly with

Connect Workers to deliver OST programs in our schools. Our program population size was 22 OST service providers, partners, and/or managers.

Data Collection

Five of the six Connect Workers conducted one-to-one interviews lasting from 45-60 minutes in length. Raw data were captured via notes during the interview verbatim and through direct quotes. Non-verbal data were also captured, and data were augmented immediately following the interview to capture the "echo effect."

Data Analysis

The Connect Workers applied a four-step model of data analysis where they focused on specific questions about the raw data within *What, How, Why, and the Heart Triangle.* After moving through this process, attention was given to identifying themes within each of the aspects.

Themes

We identified overarching themes that emerged from the full scope of the data analysis to highlight specific findings.

Quantitative Data and Analysis

We also designed a questionnaire to collect data on our quantitative indicators of impact. We sent out the survey to 22 OST service providers, and 15 responded (n=15). The responses from the surveys were collected, collated, and analyzed.

Findings

Finding 1
Strong Relationships Matter

In the Burnaby School District, Out-of-School Time (OST) service providers not only discovered that building strong relationships with

Connect Workers is beneficial for successful program delivery but that these relationships impact high-quality OST programming. Service providers in our study noticed that Connect Workers have an explicit and intentional focus on building strong and lasting relationships. Connect Workers shared that there is more "buy-in" from OST program staff where relationships between themselves and service providers are strong. Our OST partners also said they become advocates of high-quality OST programs in schools where they have significant relationships with the Connect Worker. Furthermore, service providers claimed that these strong relationships developed greater trust which allows them to reach out to Connect Workers for assistance, modeling of best practice, and mentoring.

When asked to elaborate on what trust looks like at a school with a Connect Worker, one service provider reported that "watching the Connect Worker deal with situations has given me more patience and skills with children and youth. I have developed better skills to get down to their (student) level, and staying calm in challenging situations." In the quantitative survey, 90% of service providers surveyed increased their commitment to forming strong relationships with school staff and students as a result of working with a Connect Worker. Another OST partner shared how a strong relationship between himself and the Connect Worker changed his view of his work and stated that he sees himself as a role model to children and youth rather than a Hip Hop teacher.

When asked about the value of the relationship with the Connect Worker, another OST program provider said, "There is greater impact when front-line program providers work in a building with the same Connect Worker for longer periods. There are greater trust and collaboration which helps to support higher quality programs for kids." Another partner declared that "Working together is what works best for kids and programs." This expression from the OST partner highlights the collaborative nature and student-centered focus of the model.

Significance

It is evident from our interviews and survey with OST service providers that the strength of the relationship with Connect Workers deepens their commitment to the quality of OST programming delivered. Service providers who have developed relationships to Connect Workers have more "buy in" and are stronger advocates for high-quality programs. They see themselves not only providing a service to children and youth but as a role model for developing young minds. As a result of these strong, trusting relationships with Connect Workers OST service providers are more open to collaborating, sharing information, and celebrate successes and tackle challenges.

Possible Responses

➤ Focus on the impact of positive relationships with Connect Workers and OST service providers

➤ Continue to have monthly Connect Worker meetings to explore this concept of modeling/coaching

➤ Bring all OST service providers together to build relationships and share district values

➤ Make explicit our focus on quality programming not quantity (random acts of programming)

Finding 2

Effective Communication is Key

Data showed that effective communication between Connect Workers and Out-of-School Time (OST) partners is necessary for high-quality OST programming. During an interview one of our partners reported that "Connect Workers convey relevant information about each student and assist with universal and targeted enrollment of programs to ensure that students who most need programs get in." When service providers were asked to reflect upon communication between themselves, the Connect Worker, and the school community they reported that ongoing dialogue has a positive impact on the quality of OST programs.

One service provider expressed how much she appreciated that Connect Workers share best practice in regards to dealing with vulnerable students and students with special needs. When asked to elaborate on how this communication helped her she said that "the Connect Worker has a greater knowledge about the kids' strengths and challenges and the impact of the kind of day they are having on the program they attend." She continued by saying, "Without this kind of conversation the success of the child's experience in the program would be impacted." Another OST partner claimed that his success is directly tied to the high level of information that the Connect Worker provides about the students in general, but more importantly about the day-to-day happenings for the students.

Finally, a service provider shared her appreciation that the Connect Worker connected her to the classroom teacher. The teacher incorporated some of the service provider's strategies that supported the student's social and emotional development in the program. This collaboration between the service provider and the classroom teacher supported the child's success in the classroom as well.

Significance

Effective communication between Connect Workers and OST partners is imperative for high-quality OST programming. High-quality programming cannot occur unless our service providers understand both school and community culture along with individual student needs. The Connect Workers support this focus and strive to build clear and open lines of communication.

Connect Workers share relevant information to support student success, share best practices, and assist service providers with universal and targeted enrollment to ensure program suitability for student success. Connect Workers also support direct communication between OST service providers and school staff for continued student growth and support, which impacts student success in the out-of-school hours. Without strong communication, the school and the OST programs operate as separate entities and are unable to provide each other with valuable narratives about the school, the community, and the student.

Possible Responses
- ➤ Develop a more cohesive communication plan between school staff and OST service providers
- ➤ Create "MS Office 365 Team" to generate a platform for Connect Workers to share information about program successes

Finding 3
The Gift of Building Capacity

During our interviews, we heard consistently from our Out-of-School Time (OST) partners that working alongside a Connect Worker supported their own personal and professional growth and their development and understanding of quality OST programming. One service provider reported that "Connect Workers have extensive prior knowledge about good programs and what has worked well." The OST partner felt strongly that this knowledge of high-quality programming helped him improve his program development and delivery. OST service providers expressed their appreciation for the collaborative nature of Connect Workers in their attempt to support and refine OST program goals and elements.

When asked about how working alongside a Connect Worker impacted one partner's understanding of quality programming, she reported, "We have changed the way we program and plan our after-school programs to incorporate the competencies from the redesigned curriculum." This quote highlights the role the Connect Worker plays in building capacity for program provider's ability to connect their program goals to that of BC Curriculum goals.

One partner described, "We are always exploring new avenues with programs. Changing and exploring how we can better help the children in our programs to meet the needs of each student by aligning our goals and outcomes to meet new curriculum as well as the needs of parents and their expectations of our program." These expressions from our partners highlight how this collective approach and sharing of knowledge ensures that service providers have a deeper understanding of the role they play. Another shared that Connect Workers set an example of best practice that helped him become more focused on the real reason he does "the work." He reported that his interest, passion, and encouragement of children and youth is much higher now. "I know I can provide quality programming and better yet, I know HOW to support children with the help of a Connect Worker." They are also developing an awareness of the impact of their work beyond the program they are delivering.

Significance

Working alongside a Connect Worker supports OST service providers' personal and professional growth and the development and understanding of quality programming. This helps build on our partners' knowledge of best practice in the out-of-school hours and builds capacity in our partners. Capacity building is critical to the success of our model.

The Connect Worker is intentional about passing on knowledge and strategies to support the program providers' ability to better provide quality programs. This capacity building allows the program provider to hone their skills in schools with a Connect Worker and then implement the same quality programs in schools without a Connect Worker. Service providers feel more prepared and confident to provide OST programs of higher quality across the district.

If we want all OST programs to be as effective and impactful as they are in schools where there is a Connect Worker, we must take full advantage of the skills and knowledge that each Connect Worker possesses. This then requires the Connect Worker to be intentional about sharing best practices while working alongside service providers.

Possible Responses

➢ Continued and ongoing Professional Development opportunities for Connect Workers

➢ Intentionally use Connect Worker meetings to build on their capacity so they can develop the capacity of OST staff

Finding 4
Growing Awareness of Social-Emotional Development

Overwhelmingly, Out-of-School Time (OST) service providers reported that Connect Workers help them understand the importance of developing personal and social competencies that extend beyond their program. Data from our study found that service providers gained more explicit knowledge about Social and Emotional Learning (SEL) working alongside a Connect Worker.

One partner reported, "We include social and emotional learning in all aspects of our programming as a result of what we have learned from the Connect Worker." Another reflected, "I have gained a deeper social/ emotional understanding working with an expert in the field of child and youth care." When asked about how working alongside a Connect Worker impacted partners' understanding of SEL, many service providers indicated the benefits of this dialogue. One provider said it best, "Kids are more precious to me because they are precious to Connect Workers." They reported that ongoing conversation with Connect Workers about the impact and importance of SEL helped focus the program providers' intentions of putting SEL into their OST programs.

Significance
Connect Workers work closely with the OST service providers to help build on their understanding of social and emotional learning. When programs have an explicit and intentional focus on SEL, children and youth develop greater skills in social awareness and how to better navigate in social situations. These programs pay attention to self-awareness and self-management and also build on interpersonal skills in the area of sharing, perspective taking, solving problems in peaceful ways, and care and empathy. Research suggests that OST programs that build on students'

SEL contribute to higher quality programs as students who gain greater social and emotional skills have improved attitudes about self, others, school and community, and increased positive classroom behaviours. They perform better at school academically and have fewer conduct problems. As a result, children and youth can create stronger relationships with their peers and adults in the program and show a stronger sense of belonging.

Possible Responses

- ➢ Bring OST program providers together to share district SEL goals and practice
- ➢ Professional development for Connect Workers on SEL

Finding 5

Individualized Programming Makes a Difference

Our data showed that having a deeper understanding of the unique needs of children and youth improves programming. One Out-of-School Time (OST) service provider proclaimed that working together with a Connect Worker helped her be more culturally and socially aware: "I can be more sensitive and supportive to the students…In turn, this allows me to provide a more supportive, positive, and inclusive program." When asked how working alongside a Connect Worker supported the needs of individual students, another OST provider said that they had adopted a program to include specific skills and goals for a child with special needs.

One survey participant reported, "When we were told by the Connect Worker that many of the students were new to Canada with little English language, we revamped the entire program to include more visual cues." The OST provider admitted that this would not have been the case if the Connect Worker had been involved in the enrollment selection. Seventy percent of our partners more fully embraced students' needs in their program as a result of working with a Connect Worker.

When asked about a time where individual differences were not taken into account, another OST partner recalled a program that was put together without the input from the Connect Worker. It was heavily loaded with some very challenging students with difficult behaviours. She reflected that there were significant needs and not enough staffing to support the program for those students. Another partner indicated, "The key to tailoring the program to meet the needs of individual students is by connecting with those who have strong relationships and a greater understanding...I now look for the strengths of the students and then build something that all kids will get more out of." These expressions from our OST partners indicate that when the unique needs of the individual students are taken into consideration, higher quality programming occurs.

Significance

The more understanding an OST service provider has about the unique needs of individual students, the more responsive a program is. Higher quality programs are personalized to the needs of individual students rather than merely providing generic programs. While this applies universally to all students, the Connect Worker explicitly works with service providers to build greater awareness of students with higher vulnerability. Every quality program builds on each students' unique gifts.

Possible Responses
> Work with individual schools about customizing programs for their needs (develop our process more with schools)

Finding 6
The Challenge with Turnover

During our interviews, a theme that emerged was the challenge of the high rate of turnover with Out-of-School Time (OST) program staff. A number of our partners addressed concerns that, while our Connect Workers are in the same school for many years, many OST program staff come and go. As one partner reported, "It is difficult to build relationships and deepen understanding when program staff is new each year and even each term." Another partner claimed that "there is greater impact when front-line program providers work in a building for longer periods of time to work and collaborate with the Connect Worker." Partners reported that program delivery was also impacted as a result of staff turnover.

When OST partners were asked about significant impacts of high turnover, it was reported that "Connect Workers help to prevent (staff) burn out and enable me to provide higher quality programs especially when I (program manager) have limited staffing and resources (as a result of high turnover)." Another partner indicated that "with high turnover, we couldn't deliver the program without a Connect Worker...programs run more smoothly, and we can have a greater impact on the children... we are not just going through the motions of providing a program." In some ways, it appears that the impact of the Connect Worker is even more significant in giving other staffing challenges.

Significance

A challenge for OST programs is the high rate of staff turnover. As a result, it is more difficult for Connect Workers to build strong relationships and have consistent and effective communication with program staff. This translates into lower quality programming due to the inability of sharing information consistently, modeling best practice, and engaging in ongoing and meaningful dialogue with staff. While it is beneficial to have the same Connect Worker placed in the same school for an extended period, it is challenging when the OST program staff changes regularly. Although the Connect Worker provides more stability and consistency for OST programs, the overall quality of the programs is impacted with high OST staff turnover.

Possible Responses

➢ Continue to develop our youth leadership training programs to have more youth available to work in OST programs

Conclusion and Next Steps

Next Steps

➤ Focus on the impact of positive relationships with Connect Workers and Out-of-School Time (OST) service providers

➤ Continue to have monthly Connect Worker meetings to provide professional development opportunities to focus on quality practices and Social/Emotional Learning to build on their capacity so they can develop the capacity of OST staff

➤ Bring all OST partners and service providers together annually to build relationships, share district goals about Social/Emotional Learning, and quality programming

➤ Make explicit our focus on quality programming not quantity (random acts of programming)

➤ Develop a more cohesive communication plan between school staff and OST service providers

➤ Create an "Office 365 Team" to generate a platform for Connect Workers to share information about program successes

➤ Work with individual schools about customizing programs for their needs (develop our process more with schools)

➤ Continue to develop our youth leadership training programs to have more youth available to work in OST programs

Conclusion

When Connect Workers develop strong relationships, communicate effectively, and build a shared understanding of best practice with Out-of-School Time (OST) service providers, it yields higher quality programs in schools with Connect Workers, as well as in schools without Connect Workers. In partnership with Connect Workers OST program providers understand school climate and culture, are better able to meet individual student needs, develop programs with social and emotional competencies in mind, and nurture healthy and caring relationships with students.

All of these characteristics define high-quality programs that are more than just fun activities after school. These programs are developed with intention and seek to affect multiple student outcomes. High-quality programs focus on connectedness, inclusivity, passion, and provide a supportive environment where children and youth thrive. The OST programs also pay attention to self-awareness and self-management and build on interpersonal skills.

Although these OST programs are available universally to all students, the Connect Workers work explicitly with service providers to ensure the needs of our most vulnerable students are met. Moving away from "random acts of programming" to develop programs with children and youth in mind allows for more flexible and responsive programming. The kind of programming that meets the diverse needs of vulnerable students and builds on student success. Through these kinds of high-quality programs, vulnerable children and youth can connect to a caring adult in a supportive environment, build on their interpersonal skills, master skills in areas they feel passionate about, and thrive in their school environment. As a result, our most vulnerable students have improved attitudes about themselves, others, school, and community, as well as an increase in positive school behaviours.

Vancouver School District (SD39)

Community School
TeamsYouth Leadership Program

Maggie Li, Christine Macer, Theresa Schiewe

Overview of the Organization and Program

School District #39

The Vancouver School Board is a large, urban and multicultural school district. We are committed to providing the highest quality learning experience for all students, helping them to reach their intellectual, social, and physical potential in a safe and inclusive environment. The Vancouver School District is among the most diverse public school systems in Canada with an annual enrolment of approximately 54,000 students in Kindergarten to grade 12. In addition, the Vancouver School District provides educational programs and services to full-time Adult Education students.

Community School Teams

Community School Teams are an initiative of the Vancouver School district to provide evidence-based programming which supports asset development of children and youth enrolled in Vancouver schools. Programs are developed in partnership with school and community stakeholders and are intended to support students to:

➤ Increase academic success

➤ Increase social-emotional functioning

➤ Increase community and school connectedness

➤ Increase attendance

Types of programs include but are not limited to: sports, literacy, arts and culture, food and nutrition, social-emotional skills, environmental stewardship, global citizenship, and leadership development. Many programs are low cost, participation-based and often include a 'tri-mentorship' structure with high school students and/or community members participating as volunteers.

This research project focused on the secondary students that are trained and placed in leadership roles during Out of School Time programs at elementary schools in their neighbourhood. Training and ongoing mentorship are performed by Community School Team staff who are typically young adults, many who have graduated and were previous participants as youth leaders in the Out of School Time programs.

Intended Impacts

The intended impacts of the youth leadership component of Out of School Time program include:

➤ Students realize their capacity to make a difference in the lives of others

➤ Students will become more inclusive, collaborative and adaptive problem-solvers

➤ Students will value diversity

➤ Students develop and maintain diverse positive peer and intergenerational relationships

➤ Students will develop a stronger sense of belonging to their school and community

Evaluation Methodology

Qualitative methodology
Three Vancouver Secondary schools that have a Community School Team youth leadership program were identified as the sample for this project. From each of those sites, there were a total of 430 youth leaders who were actively participating as Out of School Time volunteers. Of those 430, 41 had contributed between 60 and 100 hours of service during their tenure as a volunteer, and, were currently active in volunteering. A cross-section of these volunteers was invited to participate in an interview to discuss their experience as a volunteer (N=21). The interview team was comprised of the following: Community School Coordinator, Community School Programmer, and Manager of Community School Teams.

Description of Qualitative Analysis
Each interviewer took notes during the interviews. Notes were analyzed by individual interviewers first, then as a group to identify the findings.

Quantitative methodology
An online and paper survey was distributed to all students who were actively participating as Out of School Time volunteers during the 2017-18 school year (N=430). One hundred sixty-three surveys were completed (N=163).

Findings

Finding 1
Building Blocks of Skills

Description
Skill development was one of the features of volunteering during OST programs that were described often by youth leaders through the interviews. Our findings confirmed that through volunteer service in Community School Team programs, youth leaders report skill development in areas

of interpersonal communications, collaboration, and problem-solving. Youth demonstrate self-awareness of their strengths and areas for growth with respect to these interpersonal skills.

Interpersonal communication

It is evident that youth understand the importance of communication through the CST program. Survey responses show that youth agree (usually or always true) with the statement that they can build and maintain relationships with younger children (93%), peers (90%), and adults (70%).

> [I learnt to make] sure both sides can come to a compromise and that all parties leave feeling like the problem was resolved. And that they can continue in the program without having the problem again. It's difficult to adapt to, say it's a problem with two kids if I don't know them very well, it's difficult to come up with solutions that will satisfy everyone. It's made me think about group projects or event planning with a large group of people. It makes it easier for me to spread the work out among everyone and still consider everyone's schedule to make sure no one takes on too much.

Youth are self-aware of skills needed (listening, adaptability) to build a relationship with others:

Collaboration

Most youth associated communication as an essential skill needed in the CST program. That includes offering help with tasks, problem-solving with young children, and considering ideas of other people. They also acknowledged that being a willing collaborator to work with others is valuable in a group environment. These skills were identified by youth as an observation of a challenging experience (and reflection of said skill) while participating in our programs:

> [I learnt to have] other people helping me. The supervisors have helped me. Supervisors always keep everything smooth. [The

problem is] the kids wouldn't listen to us [the volunteers] – we asked the supervisor for help. I should be more, just let them do whatever I want – I'm really lenient – if I try to really enforce the rule then they'd listen. Yes, it applies to other aspects of my life, in group projects I just sit around and don't do much, don't give my opinion.

Based on quantitative data (N=163), youth demonstrated an understanding of the different roles they play on a team.

Figure 1. Understanding Teams

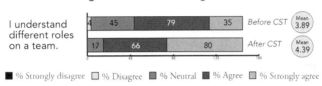

Before volunteering in the CST, 70% of surveyed youth reported that they agree or strongly agree to the statement "I understand different roles on a team"; after participating in the program, 90% agree or strongly agree to the same statement.

Problem-solving

Through working in a team environment, youth identified that they need to rely or call on help from peers, adults, and other people. Youth volunteers also acknowledged that diversity is appreciated and needed in problem-solving, which relates to Finding 4.

Figure 2. Problem Solving Skills

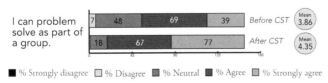

Survey data show, 88% of participants either agree or strongly agree to the statement "after participating as a CST volunteer I can problem solve as part of a group," an increase of 22% from before participation. One student reflected, "Not all problems can be solved immediately. All minds need to get together to solve one [problem]. There are always several ideas on what is the most effective and you execute it. [After volunteering,] the expectation goes higher than usual, so I ask more questions than usual when I start a new program. [For the new volunteers,] I need to explain to them about what to do." This young person gave voice to the nature of their own growth through the program.

This finding was further reinforced through responses to an open question in the survey, "The most important thing I've learned from [volunteering in] CST is…." Students' responses included,

➤ problem-solving with children with special needs
➤ How to be a part of a team to contribute to the community
➤ One can lean on other peers for help and support, and this method of completing tasks is often the most efficient way to do something
➤ How to combine individual responsibilities and tasks to form one large team that can work collaboratively to achieve a goal/run a program
➤ How to work as a team efficiently
➤ Calming conflicts, solving problems individually and in a group
➤ How to communicate with all sorts of people, from all ages

Students clearly articulated that they are developing critical problem-solving skills through their involvement.

Significance

Providing a safe environment for youth to identify, develop, and hone their skills is one of the features of the CST volunteer program. The skills that youth develop – leadership, communication, problem-solving, organization, time management, public speaking – are very translatable to the workplace. Youth leaders also identify the challenges of being accountable to the program commitments while balancing schoolwork and other responsibilities. The researchers noted that this could be a contributor to positive mental health and a deepened understanding of personal responsibility.

Youth reported using their experiences through CST leadership to better equip themselves for school group projects, in job interviews and preparation, and working with others in diverse workplaces. This reinforces our intended outcome of the CST leadership program:

> ➤ Impact #2 – students participating in CST leadership will become more inclusive, collaborative and adaptive problem solvers
> ➤ Impact #4 – students participating in CST leadership develop and maintain diverse positive peer and intergenerational relationships

Response

Self-awareness and personal responsibility were two other skills youth reported in the findings. Though insignificant in the number of survey reports, capacity building in these areas is important for youth's success in CST leadership program. Further investigation is needed to obtain a better understanding of the level of self-awareness, and personal responsibility youth think they currently have and ways that the CST staff can support development. Suggested methods include youth exit surveys, weekly reflective questions, and staff-student check-ins.

With the implementation of the redesigned curriculum in British Columbia (https://curriculum.gov.bc.ca/), there are many opportunities to embed and make explicit connections to the development of core competencies during Out of School Time programs. This opportunity will be pursued through the program planning process and will include explicit connections for youth volunteers.

Finding 2

The CST OST Programs are a Self-feeding System

Description

Youth involved in Community School Team (CST) programs as volunteers experience skill development which feeds a cycle of desire to improve and learn more. Many students indicated they began volunteering for one of two reasons: to gain the requisite hours for graduation, or because they participated in the programs as children. One student described, "Before grade 10, I didn't volunteer, and then I signed up just to do my hours but after I realized it much more than that. Of course, I will keep volunteering. I want to improve my organization [skills] and be more determined – giving up on the kids isn't an option." Another reflected, "It's a choice after 30 hours. At first, you think you just have to do it, but then you hit 30 hours, and you realize you can keep going; it's a choice." Those who reported starting in order to gain their requisite graduation hours had long since exceeded those hours; those who participated as children articulated the importance of being able to return to one's own elementary school and become leaders.

Participation as a child in the programs has impacted many to choose to volunteer when they are in secondary school. One reflected this impact, "I remember when I was like six years old listening to the leaders. Now I'm in that position teaching the kids its really made me see how much I've grown up and matured over ten years." Another described, "When I was a kid in Grade 4 in WCP[CST], I really looked up to the leaders in the program, so I said to myself 'oh when I go to high school, I'm going to join WCP', you really show kids a good example of what a good teenager is." This connection to their local community and the experience with leaders as children is a theme that emerged through the interviews across the district

The progression through various stages of volunteering and the development of skills feed they youth interest in learning more, increasing their commitment to volunteering in CST programs. One participant observed, "The more I volunteer, the more I feel comfortable working with others." Another reflected on the impact of volunteering this way, "I think through volunteering I've been able to see myself in different roles in society…I realize that I really like volunteering, it is something I hope to continue for the rest of my life. It's a nice feeling to help others and if I can inspire someone else that would be good." Ultimately this fosters a point of increased connection to their local community and often a motivator to take on volunteer roles in other organizations (Cadets, Stanley Park, City events were all noted) in different capacities.

Significance

The relationships developed among and between youth and children through the out of school time programs is not only memorable but seems to be a key component to the motivation of many youth leaders to engage as volunteers when they get to secondary school. The benefits of learning through experience in the out of school time programs, and (potentially) the progressive leadership roles that youth can take in the programs is a factor in continuing their engagement as volunteers well beyond the requisite 30 hours for graduation.

Response

The number of points of entry for engagement through Community School Team Out of School Time programs supports an asset-based community development framework which can be nourished at each of those entry points (child participant in the program, youth volunteer, youth leader, and eventually program staff) in a more explicit way.

Finding 3

Let's say it better: role modeling at school = community leadership

Description

The researchers expected to hear from youth that their involvement in CST programs gave them a sense of having a leadership role in their community. This was expected to be reflected in their descriptions of themselves and their impact and anticipated they would articulate this using language like "community" and "leadership." The qualitative data showed instead that respondents were more likely to reference role modeling in groups or specific relationships (versus a 'larger' sense of community leadership) such as, "It makes me feel like a good role model."

It is interesting to note that 90% of respondents to the quantitative survey agreed with the statement "As a result of participating in KCST, I feel I am making a positive contribution to my community." Taken with the qualitative data, this indicates that while students recognize the impact of their service, they don't yet articulate it as leadership.

Figure 3. Contributing to the Community

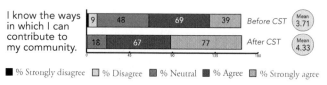

There were a minority of qualitative data points that showed an exception to this theme: each of these had to do with a student who spoke about other service work they do outside of school. Students who talked about their involvement in non-school volunteer and job placements did reference larger themes of "community" and "leadership."

They were able to describe themselves as leaders within the community, without having to specify a specific group or geographic place. Students with varied volunteer experience said things like: "I also volunteer in day camps and Canucks Autism Network. [My community service benefits] parents, kids, and other volunteers." Again, this is in contrast to students who only had Community School Team experience, who tended to only describe themselves as leaders or role models in a school context.

Significance
An individual's ability to fully use their skills and role requires a keen self-awareness of both their skills and their sphere of influence. We can see that if we can help students reframe and more fully understand the impact and scope of their volunteer role, they would develop greater self-awareness - and therefore greater capacity to act.

Response
There is an opportunity to help students understand that role modeling is one part of leadership – and that they are also practicing other related

skills (giving direction, managing group behaviour, motivating others). Secondly, staff needs to help students understand that by working with small groups of children, they are acting within the larger scope of their community - impacting the students, their families, and other stakeholders in the school environment. Simply put, staff need to help students recognize that being a school leader is being a community leader.

Finding 4
Identifying Diversity or Problem-Solving Differences?

Description
One of the intended impacts of the CST program for youth leaders is to value diversity and demonstrate respectful and inclusive behaviour. The researchers expected to see that youth are discovering and identifying diversity through the participating in the program and in turn, learning how to cater to other learning needs of either children or their peers. However, this evaluation identified that there needs to be a better understanding of educating the concept of or recognizing the value of diversity in the CST programs.

The qualitative question designed to explore diversity was "what have you discovered about the ways people can be different? How has this learning influenced you?". The researchers were surprised that the youth responses focused on the need for solving problems because of differences amongst the young children, and not necessarily the acknowledgment and appreciation of such differences. For example, one youth said,

> Everyone has their differences, and one thing I usually do is try to find similarities between everyone to help bond everyone together. Everyone's different, and everyone needs to be treated differently, but fairly. I guess I try to find the version of how I want to be treated with them. I guess talking about differences with people it usually ends up positive because it's a good way to come up with solutions to problems.

The word different was often used for youth to describe observations or experiences that required problem-solving. One student observed, "You [...] can learn about how they are different from you. That it is OK for people to be different and think different from you and we can all get along. It's OK to be different. Some kids can be more chill; some may have anger issues...I treat them the same, but some may need more help...I can respond to those needs." In turn, youth described the skills required to connect with an individual child which included: patience, courage, communication, working with peers (who may not necessarily be friends), understanding different points of view.

In the quantitative surveys, the question designed to measure diversity was "as a result of participating in CST, I appreciate groups with a mix of strengths, interests, needs, and identities." Over 85% of youth reported that this statement is usually or always true. Unlike the quantitative survey statement, the qualitative question of "what have you discovered about the ways people can be different? How has this learning influenced you?" is more neutral in tone; thus generated an open-ended discussion. The youth had a difficulty articulating the concept of diversity during the qualitative interviews; we contributed the findings to the vagueness in our design question and youth inability to articulate and identify diversity as a positive value.

Significance

In the CST program, having a mutual understanding of the strength of diversity fosters better conflict resolution skills and improved respect and recognition. Youth leaders, through the CST program, are identifying that young children have different learning styles, and peers have a variety of viewpoints in problem-solving. However, the respondents' association of diversity with the need to problem solve was surprising in the findings and led to the researchers to reflect on the interview question design, as well as the need to highlight diversity as a positive concept in our program design.

Response

CST programs aim to contribute to creating an environment where youth can appreciate and respect diverse perspectives, and youth can share that value to young children where it is "okay to be themselves and create what they like" in CST programs. This positivity around diversity is central to CST programs and aligns with the Vancouver School District mission "to enable students to reach their intellectual, social, aesthetic and physical potential in challenging and stimulating settings which reflect the worth of each individual and promote mutual respect, cooperation, and social responsibility" (https://www.vsb.bc.ca/District/Pages/default.aspx).

Diversity, or "different kind of smarts," should be intentionally promoted or integrated into CST programs. A beginning step would be to include a reflective discussion question celebrating diversity for youth leaders. An example could be "give a shout-out to someone who had a unique activity idea or unique way of program solving during the programs today that you would otherwise not think about." Also, further design in quantitative and qualitative data collection questions is needed to understand youth leaders' perspectives on inclusion and diversity more fully and accurately.

Finding 5

Happiness is…

Description

For the youth interviewed, most identified a feeling of happiness from interacting with and seeing the children registered in the program on a weekly basis. One youth expressed, "The best part about being a youth leader is seeing the kids smile and that makes [me] happy." Through the interviews, many responses led back to the experience with children and how motivating, inspiring, and despite frustrations the key element which maintained commitment over a school year or multiple years as a volunteer.

This finding is tied very closely with finding 6 – all but two youth who participated in interviews articulated a feeling of happiness related to spending time with the children on a weekly basis, and/or the sense of responsibility that they felt to follow through on their commitment to be in the programs as scheduled. 76% of youth responded that the following statement is usually or always true: "As a result of participating in CST, I can lead programs in such a way that all younger students can say 'I belong here'." This again points to the importance of the peer relationships youth are developing with children through the CST programs.

Significance

That youth report a feeling of happiness from regular engagement with a group of children is an implicit part of the program and thus its impact was unexpected. Youth reported feeling a sense of responsibility but of also wanting to ensure they were their "best self" as role models and able to play with the children while leading them. One youth shared, "Best part [of volunteering] is seeing the kids happy, because when they're happy you're happy. It's a good feeling. Whenever I think of the kids, I am happy, and I remember what I learned from them." Working with children was also noted as one of the frustrations. However, the frustrations seemed to be perceived as much smaller than the feelings of happiness that resulted through the development of relationships with children.

Response

Increase the explicit information to community stakeholders as anxiety and mental health is an increasing concern among educators leveraging the research that demonstrates that happiness is an antidote to anxiety.

Finding 6

"They expect ME."

Description

The researchers heard loud and clear from youth respondents that a key motivating factor in their continued involvement (and personal investment of time) was the elementary students expecting them as individuals to come each program day. One youth leader stated, "The kids motivate me because it's not fair to them if I don't show up." The youth specifically articulated that they felt needed – the elementary students didn't just expect a volunteer, they expected them personally: "…you have a responsibility to be there, those kids are waiting on you." The impact of being needed on the youth's commitment was compelling.

The youth respondents were also able to articulate the feelings of the younger children in this dynamic: "And for the kids […] It makes them realize that high school students are there for them and will be there for them." Another student shared, "I know if I commit to it then the kids will know someone is committing to them." The quantitative data also reflected the youth leaders' understanding of their relationships with children: 93% of youth leaders chose "Always True" or "Usually True" in response to the statement, "As a result of participating in CST, I can build and maintain relationships with younger children."

Significance

The relationship youth develop with younger peers is perhaps the most significant factor in a youth continuing to devote time and be consistent in honouring their volunteer commitment. The data lead the researchers to consider how the volunteer experience with children in their neighbourhood may impact: the youth's positive self-identity, relationship-building skills overall, and development of personal intrinsic value.

Response

Staff can use this finding to bolster recruitment and retention strategies by focusing on supporting youth leaders in developing relationships with children in the programs. This also creates future opportunities for more intentional education of the youth leaders. Using the Social-Emotional Learning (SEL) curriculum in CST volunteer training. Secondly, staff can integrate BC Ministry of Education Core Competencies (specifically, the Personal and Social competencies) into the volunteer training and support to help youth learn to articulate their skills in relationship building and help translate these skills to other key areas of their lives.

Conclusion and Next Steps

Conclusion

The impact of the CST youth leadership experience on the participants can indeed support their overall skill development and connection to their community (both to individuals and their feeling of belonging). The unanticipated responses, especially regarding happiness and connectedness to the children whom they were leading are areas for future development. There is strong evidence through this evaluation to both continue the CST youth leadership program, and more importantly, use the recommendations above to strengthen it. The existing structures are a strong foundation upon which to build this experience for Vancouver students.

Next Steps

➤ Make the implicit explicit. If an intended outcome or impact is skill development, identify them clearly and find opportunities to embed that into the training and volunteer experience. Use of the BC Curriculum language on Core Competencies and the "I can" statements through the youth volunteer training, program plans for OST, and reflection exercises for youth leaders.

➤ Make explicit connections for youth regarding diversity in all forms and articulate through training, modeling, and experience why understanding and supporting diversity is important.

➤ Build on the happiness that youth reported feeling as a result of their experience. Promote this widely to stakeholders in the program, including and most importantly, youth in Secondary schools.

➤ Ensure that youth voice through reflection and evaluation s incorporated more formally into the Out of School Time youth volunteer experience; gather quantitative and qualitative data on an annual basis.

United Way of the Lower Mainland

Lower Mainland Out of
School Time Alliance (LMOST)

Maggie Karpilovski, Dan Marriott

Introduction

Program

The LMOST (Lower Mainland Out of School Time) Alliance is an initiative of United Way of the Lower Mainland (UWLM). Beginning in 2012, a group of UWLM funded Community School Partnership leaders along with ministry representatives and UWLM staff began to meet quarterly to discuss common efforts, challenges, and opportunities in Out of School Time (OST) programs. LMOST's foremost purpose is to advocate and promote quality OST programs.

Vision

The LMOST Alliance works to promote quality out-of-school time programs (OST).

Mission

To engage organizations to increase quality out-of-school time program initiatives in schools and communities.

Goals

➢ Be an effective voice for OSTs in an effort to expand quality programs.
➢ Serve as an information source on OST programs and resources.
➢ Encourage the development of quality OST systems.
➢ Communicate the impact of OST programs on children, families, and communities.
➢ Increase understanding of the value of OST programs.

Initiatives

➢ Identify innovative and evidence-informed practices through sharing and research.
➢ Increase the capacity, knowledge, and skills of community-based providers through the sharing of resources.
➢ Work together to become a credible voice for the promotion of quality OSTs and advance policy change.
➢ Strengthen cross-sectorial partnerships to maximize outcomes.
➢ Utilize expertise and knowledge from the community to support the learning and well-being of young people.
➢ Promote understanding of the value of OST programs among parents, schools, and community.

Since the time of its inception the LMOST Alliance has expanded its reach to 3 more School Districts and grown to include representatives from local Universities.

Recently, the LMOST Alliance, with the support of UWLM, has co-sponsored two major conferences (Symposium 2016 and Summit 2018). The events brought together players from the OST community including key stakeholders, service providers, and community partners to present research and ideas about OSTs across North America. Finally, a recent partnership with Simon Fraser University has resulted in a research arm of LMOST to assist with major grant funding opportunities.

More information about LMOST can be found at **http://www. lmost.org.**

Evaluation Methodology

The LMOST Alliance as a sector strengthening, capacity building initiative, is part of UWLM's significant investment into children aged 6-12. The initiatives include a funding stream for Out of School Time programs (School's Out) and funding for local Districts to support Community School Partnerships. Other capacity building activities within this investment stream include a community of practice for UWLM School's Out funded agencies.

As the landscape of OST across BC evolves, we sought to evaluate the impact of LMOST through a broad lens of capacity building activities within the OST sector in the lower mainland. We used a developmental evaluation to focus on improving the activities offered.

Through the Project Impact process, we identified a set of impacts to guide the evaluation:

➤ OST Providers are delivering intentional, high-quality programming.

➤ Decision makers at different levels of governance support OST programming through effective collaboration.

➤ The OST stakeholder community is informed about OST offerings, benefits and have confidence in the delivery of OST programs.

Led by the expert direction of DIalogues in Action and generously sponsored by UWLM, our team consisted of a Middle-Years planner from the UWLM and the coordinator of LMOST.

Qualitative Methodology

An interview protocol comprised of eleven questions was developed through the Project Impact process. The team developed a random, stratified sample of interviewees from three distinct groups: members of the Community Schools Partnership (directly part of LMOST until 2018); members of School's Out Community of Practice; and; attendees of Summit 2018.

The team conducted interviews over a two- week period immediately following the Summit 2018 (May 25, 2018). In total, 18 interviews were conducted with participants from all three categories. Interviewee notes were the basis of the data corpus, where possible, interviews were also recorded. Recordings were transcribed for accuracy and combined with the notes, and approximately 200 pages of data were available for analysis. A theme map was developed based on multiple readings of the data, and as themes emerged, the team analyzed the quantitative data for confirmatory or contradicting findings.

Quantitative Methodology

A quantitative questionnaire was created to survey Summit 2018 participants. The purpose of the questionnaire was to gauge the changes in participant views before and after the Summit. Eighteen questions were composed, with the first 14 questions asking respondents to measure their responses on a five-point Likert scale; before and following the Summit with the intention of measuring its effectiveness. The next series of questions asked participants to prioritize work emphasis and rank significance of various aspects of OST programmes. Finally, respondents were asked to write about the impact of OST and the quality of OST programmes.

Seventy-one (N=71) questionnaires were completed and collected. Each survey was numbered for tabulation and tracking input purposes. All Likert scale responses were added to a spreadsheet for analysis. Responses to the remaining questions were compiled thematically in a narrative format.

Findings

Finding 1
It's all Social

Description

While interviewees reported highly valuing the opportunity to network within UWLM supported initiatives such as the OST summit, LMOST table, and the School's Out Community of Practice, networking was not the intention but the by-product. Many expressed the desire to have a focus on networking as a prime goal.

The inherent nature of working in and with community is to work with groups of people. Creating and producing programs for a community is a group process. Data show that among practitioners, networking is seen as a valuable method for garnering relationships leading to a common vision for children and families. One practitioner described, "I find the networking piece of that really helpful to be able to be directly connected to similar roles as myself but across districts. That portion has been really helpful." Networking is seen as an initial process for achieving goals.

Significance

Although UWLM's investment in programmed content for professional development and sector strengthening is important and an effective strategy, practitioners seek networking opportunities as an initial step towards collaboration, aligning their interests, finding allies and building a circle of supportive colleagues. As one described one "can't do it on your own and you need that network of support. I need those mentors in my life."

The importance of networking also appears in the data collected from the survey following Summit 2018. One question asked whether participants felt closer to their colleagues following the Summit. Of the respondents, 46% showed an increasingly positive trend. In a subsequent question, 43% of respondents indicated that events like the summit increased their collaboration opportunities.

Responses

Recognizing the need to support networking as an independent initiative, we recommend the establishment of a Networking Committee for the planning and execution of social events. We also recommend a feasibility study to explore a dedicated social media platform to allow colleagues to connect online.

Finding 2

ColLABORation

Description

Many participants identified the importance of collaboration in their work. It was also recognised that collaboration is a scaffolded process with ambiguous stages of development. A notable challenge is identifying the stage of collaboration in an active environment.

Practitioners' use of the term "collaboration" is a reflection of their personal experiences working with others as a unit. UWLM has supported structural and event initiatives to host and promote the collaborative developmental process across its grant streams for several years. LMOST and School's Out Communities of Practice have provided structures for collaboration, and the Summit has offered international examples of what developed collaboration can render for communities.

LMOST, as a UWLM sponsored initiative, is viewed as a supporting structure. LMOST is a model of cross-sectoral collaboration whose purpose is to promote the value of quality OST programs. The stakeholders have the common goal of OST programs as their binding vision. Data reveal that OST practitioners see the value in LMOST in several ways, both as a platform and gateway to relevant research and as a format for networking and collaboration. LMOST has provided the opportunity for networking, raised awareness of relevant research on OST programs, and co-sponsored research-oriented events (Summit 2018 and Symposium 2016).

The Summit 2018 was a UWLM sponsored event bringing together international researchers to describe collaborative programs, illustrating research relevant to the significance of OSTs. Data collected from participants of the Summit emphasized the importance of collaboration. One reflected, "Well, understanding the research presented at the Summit is helpful in advocacy. Understanding the provincial context, as well as a regional context and making connections within those contexts." The graphs below illustrate the very strong agreement that cross-sectoral collaboration is important for OST programming. Following the Summit, nearly all respondents either agreed or strongly agreed that cross-sectoral collaboration is important in the field of OST programs.

Figure 1. Responses to the statement
"Effective cross-sectoral collaboration is important
in the OST field."

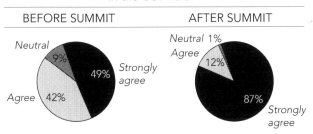

Through networking experiences from the above initiatives, OST practitioners have developed relationships which can be described as the beginning stages of collaboration. We have found that what collaboration means to each practitioner varies between utility, relationships, and barriers.

Utility

Many participants reported on the utility of developing partnerships for collaboration specifically to increase resource access. This is mostly driven by the lack of resources – facilities, funding, and training for staff. As one described, "Collaboration and partnerships are really key for grant applications for doing more with less."

In addition to interview data, the Summit survey also provided an opportunity for participants to reflect on collaborative possibilities.

see chart on next page

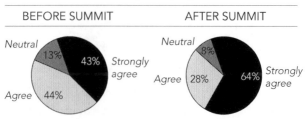

Figure 2. Responses to the statement
"I see opportunities to collaborate for the
benefit of my OST programs."

Following the Summit, respondents indicated a shift from a neutral or positive response to a much more positive response following the Summit. After the Summit, 92% agreed or strongly agreed that they see further opportunities for collaboration.

Relationships

Networking and social interactions are the basis for initially forming relationships which create a foundation for collaboration. In many instances, relationships are the glue that holds partnerships and a collaborative group together. One attendee noted, "That's probably at the foremost for us is that real sense of building relationships and strong partnerships between the district and the schools and the service providers."

Barriers

All participants have indicated support for collaboration, however, also stated that challenges to collaboration include competing interests such as conflicting mandates and time. One practitioner described, "Yeah, collaboration is time-consuming….. It's hard collaborating with other agencies who have different mandates, and it's, just takes more time when you have to hear back from five people, compared to just talking to the person in my office, you know, when we have five minutes. Yeah, that's something that we ... it's challenging. It's important, but it's challenging." A significant personal challenge described by OST practitioners is their threshold of personal frustration with regard to the implementation challenges.

Significance

Although programmed content for professional development and sector strengthening are important and effective strategies, practitioners seek networking opportunities as an initial step towards collaboration. Research literature has described stages of collaboration development (Weick, 1979). As groups evolve through stages, "becoming social" is one of the benchmarks. Our concern for those seeking collaboration is not to "get stuck" in that phase, inhibiting further development. Supportive structures such as LMOST and the Summit provide key components to instantiating collaboration, providing a venue for common understanding. These events act as catalysts for motivation.

While LMOST has helped to standardize a language around OST, UWLM initiatives have created the beginning structures as models for future development. There is always a need for further development. One participant described, "I see, a bit of a role for LMOST is how they could support in terms of a research piece, a very simplistic what is OST; here's some highlights that research; this is what drives it; this is the philosophy behind it so that we have a starting point. Then everybody can grow their own from their community perspective." To become mature collaborative structures, partners involved need to share resources and governance models.

Responses

As collaboration is still a developing process, we recommend LMOST focus on the following;

> ➤ Training and scaffolding partners through the stages of development.
> ➤ Highlight groups that are already engaged in collaboration to describe their benchmarks/thresholds.
> ➤ Explicate benefits of collaboration.
> ➤ Highlight LMOST as a collaborative example.

Finding 3

Quality is not a dirty word

Description

Efforts of UWLM initiatives to focus on program quality have resulted in a broader scope of discussion within the field of OST practitioners. Despite this, OST program quality needs to be explained and exemplified for greater understanding and adoption by practitioners.

Respondent data reveal that while OST practitioners aim for quality programming, there is a lack of common understanding or definition of criteria to support program evaluation. On practitioner reflected, "I'd love to know more about the quality piece, like what do we truly know about what makes a quality experience for children and the benefits." Another described, "we need to be really intentional about how we're monitoring the quality. I think it's a topic that people have a hard time defining." The focus on quality as a key takeaway from the summit was corroborated by the survey data. When asked if respondents were motivated to focus on quality in their OST programs, 78% of respondents indicated being more committed to quality standards following the summit. This compares to only 49% before the summit.

Practitioners want to expend resources on programs that are effective and lead to high-quality outcomes. To achieve those goals, practitioners need specific definitions of quality to measure their efficacy. One shared, "[My wish] is digging into quality measures. And I know that we have meta-analyses. We have data we can draw on. But putting that into a consumable, digestible, pragmatic format that we could adopt as a region regarding the inputs." As evident from the interview data, quality, as it is self-perceived, can also become a barrier in the absence of a clear, discernable definition. As well, the data point to a definite desire to gain greater understanding and utility of measures of quality. The term quality is ubiquitous. Interviewees used the term frequently applied to many different areas. Often quality programs are equated with quality staff. That does not define a quality program, only shifts the need to define quality staff for a program. If the equivocation between high-quality staff and high level of training is present, the implications for having highly trained program leaders is enormous. Standards, training thresholds, remuneration, and advancement are a few of the personnel issues that standardized, high-quality staff.

In addition, quality programs were often equated with high-quality outcomes. One participant described, "'Quality program(s)' is always mentioned as a pathway to achieve positive outcomes, justify expenditures, leverage grant funding and meet the needs of the community in a satisfying manner." This implies that those outcomes are measurable and are in place prior to the program starting.

Significance

Quality needs to be changed from a concept to a construct through explication by defining measurable and achievable goals and universally understood standards. Evaluation criteria would be supported by a benchmark for program definition, professionalization and standardization of the field, elevating the level of service provision sector-wide.

Responses

Quality is a key priority for LMOST - to that end we recommend more efforts be put in place to move quality from concept to construct for OST practitioners. This could be achieved by the adoption of consistent standards for program delivery matched to training opportunities and accreditation programs.

Finding 4

The E in LOVE

Description

The OST providers' sector is full of passionate and dedicated people. One practitioner shared, "I've always loved my work. I'm very passionate about my work. I love just to mentor and coach and whatever I learn, I just like to bring it in and kind of share it with others." UWLM initiatives provide an avenue for evoking passion and driving energy to carry on the work with children, family, and youth by OST practitioners.

Passion for working with the community is a compelling force for practitioners to not only persevere but to succeed. Survey data showed that practitioners are strongly committed to their jobs and that commitment surfaces as a strong emotional investment in their work. When asked what emotion do you experience when you work in your community, a wide range was reported. It was striking to notice the depth of the emotional commitment practitioners felt. One shared, "I always say the job that I'm in, I feel like it was handmade for me. It's all the things that I'm extremely passionate about. It's the work that I love to do most, so I have a real sense of purpose." Finding the right person for the right job is always imperative, but none more than working with the community through diverse needs and complex relationships. Most reported positive emotions such as happiness, passion, and joy. As one interviewee pointed out, the significance of their work is not reflected in remuneration; but the "life-changing" nature of the work.

Unfortunately, barriers in the work can also cause anxiety and stress. Several interviewees commented on "anxiety" as part of a community developmental process, and the personal "stress" characteristics (sore neck and shoulders) to which is atypical in other lines of work. One participant reflected, "Then there's, I guess, a little bit of anxiety and then there's that like, 'Ah-ha,' where it starts to fall into place and all starts to come together. I guess a whole range of emotions." Emotional investment can work both ways: deep satisfaction; and; deep anxiety.

Significance

While working with community comes with inherent emotional rewards, it can also take a personal toll. The challenges of working closely with a community must be a consideration for all future and current practitioners.

Responses

To support practitioner well-being, we recommend creating tools that support resilience, including peer mentorship groups and HR support for smaller organizations.

Finding 5

Don't A-ssume; T-est, A-nalyze

Description

LMOST and UWLM initiatives have created opportunities to access and interpret key research in the area of OST, increasing the use of research data in the practitioner community for program improvement.

Research-based practice initiatives have taken a key role in guiding purposeful change for OST practitioners. Research evidence provides direction based on analytic trends but must be derived from credible and robust resources. As the practitioners are becoming better consumers of information, the ability to determine the validity of a study has improved. Survey participants reported that their ability to share good knowledge, based on data, was supporting their programs in a variety of ways. It is encouraging them to:

➢ Advocate and promote their programs to grow partnerships.

"I think it's definitely the research behind it. It's what I have found most beneficial. Just to be able to hear the context of the research, to be able to know that there is sound research being done around OST, the benefits of OST for children."

➢ Achieve funding support for programs.

"Grant writing, I would say, is a portion of that, being able to be accountable and to be able to collect relevant data to make sure that we can justify and be accountable for our funds and to show where those funds are going and the gain and the benefit of those funds."

➤ Leverage support other than financial, including awareness and recognition of the impact of OSTs by decision makers, increases overall community support, endorsing both credibility and legitimacy.

"I think what it does though is give me tools when I'm talking to other people about OST and its importance. So, the research that comes out I can then share with our superintendent and with our funders and can say, 'Hey, this is why it's important. Support it.' And it's worked really well. That piece has been great."

➤ A theoretical scaffold - Increasing understanding supports the "why" of OSTs.

"…for me, if I can understand the why behind something, then it fuels my philosophical understanding to then move forward. It feeds the passion. I've really enjoyed learning more about the research, and I'd love to know more about the quality piece, like what do we truly know about what makes a quality experience for children and the benefits."

The foregoing examples illustrate multiple ways in which OST practitioners have used data as a means to support and grow their work.

Significance
Data-informed decisions offer reliability and can be trusted to drive program improvement activities. Recognition of quality research is a growing need among those less familiar with the utility of data. Practitioners need to focus on interpreting research data considering how it can be used in their organizations. Recognizing quality research and understanding its utility are new roles for OST practitioners. Data in and of itself is not sufficient, but combined with meaning-making protocols and intentional, objective

program evaluation processes can affect meaningfully change. Evaluation data should be intentionally and continuously analyzed to drive decisions around program improvement.

Responses

Based on the survey findings of positive trends towards increased usage of research for program advancement, we recommend continued support for the Community Scholars portal with more training and support opportunities.

Finding 6

Small cog in a big wheel

Key insight

The Summit, as well as other UWLM initiatives, have provided a view and reference point for the participants' place in the larger picture of OSTs, providing a way to finding meaning in their work. These events complement their passion, driving engagement in their work to meet the needs of children and families

Summit participants gained insight and awareness into their position and how they fit into the OST landscape. One described, "My role is to inspire my team, help them understand what the big picture is and how their piece applies to it...It made me realize what a huge impact it has." Another reflected, "You kind of can easily miss that bigger picture, so I think just moving forward with it, again, it gives these small steps are steps to complete that bigger picture, that bigger goal, so it's kind of a marathon, we're not in it for the sprint." Knowing you are not alone in your work connects practitioners to a community.

Answers to question 2 (below) show that prior to the Summit, the majority of participants indicated they felt connected to their colleagues: 61% either agreed or strongly agreed that they felt connected to their colleagues.

see chart on next page

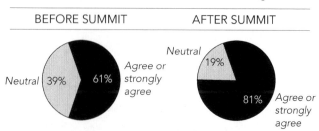

Figure 3. Responses to the statement
"I feel better connected to other OST colleagues."

Following the Summit, more participants felt greater connections: 80% either agreed or strongly agreed that they felt connected to their colleagues.

OST Practitioners described the experience as being part of the solution to a puzzle, supporting the foundational underpinnings of their work. One participant described, "It's those pieces of the puzzle that kinda come together that creates that more wider picture of the work that we're doing." The Summit seems to facilitate the work of putting the pieces together.

Significance

Awareness of an OST practitioners' role in the OST landscape supports engagement and fulfillment leading to personal satisfaction, one of the four core needs for employees according to studies conducted by the Energy Group and Harvard University (Schwartz and Porath, NYT, May 30, 2014). The role of LMOST is to help practitioners to understand the puzzle and people's role within that.

Responses

We recommend continuing with the Summit every 2-3 years to help practitioners maintain awareness of the OST provision landscape, including a knowledge mobilization initiative demonstrating the use of a Community Development Map and where OST programs fit into the development of children and communities.

Finding 7
Educating the Heart

Description

There are many benefits to OST programs, from skill development to scaffolding positive peer relationships. The wide variety of OST programs supported by UWLM exemplify the range of potential program focus areas. Summit participants were asked to "Select three elements that you consider the most important for OST programs." Three topics stood out as significant priorities before and after the Summit: safety; connection with an important adult; and; social and emotional development.

The graph below illustrates the changes in the three major aspects as indicated by Summit participants.

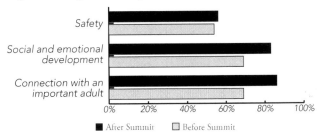

Figure 4. Program Priority Shift Before and After Summit

Respondents indicated that safety was significant before and after the Summit - 55% and 56% respectively, illustrating that participants felt that safety of children is omnipresent. The other two aspects showed positive trends, and reflect the impact of presentations and discussions during the Summit. Both social and emotional development and connection to an important adult increased significantly: 14% and 17% respectively.

The Summit experience influenced the shift in the significance of program priorities for many participants. One participant reflected, "We're focusing on social-emotional learning. I feel like the summit ... It just reminded me of things, like sometimes programming ideas or things that you just haven't had a chance to get to. So kind of helps reboot or reset the structure a little bit I think for our program." It seems to have encouraged more focus on Social and Emotional Development; and; connections to important adults in the child's world.

Significance

Compelling, quality research coupled with knowledgeable presenters can influence program priorities. Large-scale gatherings of practitioners where ideas are presented with fact-based information can render changes in either program emphasis or direction. These plenary-type sessions coupled with highly interactive small group discussions, like Summit 2018, have implications for resources: material; training; funding and facilities. Once practitioners have accepted the necessity to adopt a change and want to act on that change, there will be a need for a similar shift in resource emphasis as well.

Specifically, for OST programs, a shift in significance rendered by the data indicate that there will be a greater need for training program leaders in the Social and Emotional Development of children and the role of program leader as possibly the "important adult" in children's lives. Training with an emphasis on the importance of relationships and trust based on positive role modelling will be imperative in shifting program priorities.

Responses

We recommend capitalizing on the shift that is happening and increase in-service training on Social and Emotional Development for OST practitioners - preferably in a collaborative fashion - using existing structures and local expertise. Additionally, we recommend creating standards for training and ongoing technical assistance for existing program leaders.

Conclusion and Next Steps

The impacts of LMOST and United Way initiatives are readily found in the data from both the qualitative and quantitative data sets rendered from OST practitioners. Key impacts the team discovered appear as:

> ➤ Structured modelling, offering scaffolds for support; providing positive platforms for collaboration.

- ➤ Resources for relevant research, discussions, and presentations that are highly valued for networking and knowledge mobilization.
- ➤ Connectivity for the community of practitioners to draw meaning and place-finding in their work.

Recommendations flowing from our findings are all plausible action items that will continue to support and improve the work of OST practitioners.

The continued work of LMOST and UW initiatives will incorporate not only the recommendations but also a structure for reflective evaluation. Intentional and purposeful reflective actions will benefit future work of LMOST and UWLM initiatives.

Surrey School District

Attendance Matters

James Speidel, Mark Elke, Rani Gandham,
Zoe Makrigiannis, Meredith Verma

Organization and Program Overview

The Surrey School District was formed in 1906 and has the largest enrollment in the province with approximately 73,000 students. It currently is made up of 106 Elementary schools, 21 Secondary Schools and 5 District Learning Centres.

Community Schools Partnership (CSP) is a district department as part of School and Community Connections, which encompasses two additional departments of Safe Schools and the Welcome Centre. CSP works in collaboration with schools to address vulnerabilities and create targeted opportunities before, during and after school for all children to reach their full potential, expand their learning and grow socially and emotionally. CSP works together with community agencies, partners, various funders, and district departments to build capacity within schools and create meaningful opportunities that scaffolds support for at-risk student populations.

This is accomplished by CSP staff working together with schools to identify specific needs of children and families. From a strategic planning perspective, our department intends to create collaborative, intentional and sustainable programming to meet the needs of all of our learners and further support lifelong learning.

Community Schools Partnership offers Attendance Matters (AM), which is one of our signature programs in the morning portion of the school day and which is the focus of this study. Furthermore, CSP has various Lunchtime programs that focus on Physical Literacy and Mentorship and a variety of After School Programs in both the Elementary and Secondary level. These programs run in our schools during the critical care hours of Out of School Time (OST) hours, which includes before, during and after school. In total, we service over 60 schools within our District. In addition, CSP works together with Community Organizations to facilitate supportive learning programs to other school locations throughout the district. As a department, our community partners and strategic relationships maximize our degree of impact for our students and value these collaborative partnerships.

Community Schools Partnership has six intended impacts that serve as a guidepost to bring intentionality in all our programs.

> ➢ Children are ready, able, and motivated to learn
> ➢ Children are experiencing enriched and expanded learning.
> ➢ Children are building resiliency, hope and expanding horizons.
> ➢ Families are engaged in their children's learning
> ➢ Schools, families, and children are connected to a continuum of support for their needs.
> ➢ The community is involved in collaborative partnerships to support learning.

Description of Program

Attendance Matters began as a pilot program in September 2010/2011 in one inner-city elementary school in the north of Surrey. The goal of the program was to support students with their social/emotional connection to school which was supplemented with breakfast to draw in students to arrive at school on time. Current research on attendance shows that students who with more than 2 - 3 unexcused absences a month (18 - 27 per year), have a challenging time 'catching up' and long-term are impacted socially and academically by those absences.

Poor attendance has serious implications for later outcomes as well… high school [students who show] high levels of absenteeism throughout their childhood… observed as early as kindergarten, and students who eventually dropped out of high school missed significantly more days of school in first grade than their peers who graduated from high school. (Hickman, 2007)

It is well documented is that school districts that implement high-quality attendance programs with the support of relationships create a significant impact on student attendance and student achievement.

Since 2010, the increasing demand for attendance monitoring and data collection has continued as our school population and city continues to grow. In 2010, our district had just over 62,000 students. The student population has grown to just over 72,000 in 2018. The increase in student numbers brings an increase in school programs, services and funding. It has become a significant focus of our district goals to have every student cross the stage and graduate with dignity and purpose. The Attendance Matters (AM) program has grown over the last 8 years to include twenty-three elementary schools in 2018.

The AM program supports students identified as having high rates of absence/tardiness to attend school on a more regular basis. This is done by wrapping outreach services around students and families as well as encouraging students to attend the breakfast program at their school each morning. Here, students are provided with a warm and healthy morning meal and are engaged in literacy-focused games and activities before beginning their school day. At some sites, students are also involved in physical recreation activities in the school gym after they finish eating breakfast. With primary students (K-3), the focus of AM includes the role of the outreach staff developing and maintaining relationships with school staff, students and families. They liaise with school staff to support students and families in having good attendance habits.

CSP staff or Outreach Workers (Ow's) have an identified group of primary (K-3) students who are chronically absent (10% absenteeism or higher) or consistently late for school. Between the hours of 7:30am-9: 30

am, outreach staff uses a variety of methods to support student attendance. This includes (but is not limited to):

> - wake-up calls,
> - door knocks,
> - pick-ups (temporary basis/emergency situations),
> - follow-up calls,
> - encouraging students to attend the breakfast club, and
> - checking in with students within the school.

By providing this extra layer of support, the outreach staff helps children and families to build resiliency and more responsible habits that will serve them over the long term.

A robust partnership with Simon Fraser University has enabled further research into chronic absenteeism. Between 9:00am-10: 00 am, outreach staff contact families who have had a primary student (K-3) absent the day prior in hopes of conducting a survey. Research into understanding the definitions, causes, and interventions associated with chronic absenteeism is crucial in promoting district understandings and possibly informing district policy into effectively addressing the issue.

Evaluation Methodology

The purpose of our evaluation was to explore the scope and quality of our intended impacts of the AM program and the students and families. During this period, we

> - Evaluated and refined our ideas of intended impact and indicators,
> - Designed and implemented both qualitative and quantitative means to collect and analyze data, and
> - Identified findings and considered the implications of these findings for program adjustments and additions.

This evaluative process began with a focus on identifying and clarifying the intended impact, roles, and approaches that were being used to support identified students' attendance.

Once the ideas had been developed, and indicators identified, we designed an interview protocol to collect qualitative data from a representative sample of Outreach Workers (OW) that facilitate the AM program as well as parents of students who either were currently in the program or had participated within the last year. A questionnaire was developed to assess quantitative measures to convey a complete picture of the results. This data were analyzed, themes identified and then translated into findings. From the findings, we learned useful program insights that will impact and support decisions for continued improvement, development, and enhancement of the program going forward.

Qualitative Data Collection and Analysis
Our qualitative approach included the six main components described here.

Protocol Design
We designed an in-depth interview protocol using the Heart Triangle method of question construction. This produced 12 questions based on the three intended impacts that were formulated specifically for AM. (See chart below). Each intended impact had a total of four questions, with a minimum of 3 questions being asked under each impact. The protocol was our guide to collect data about the staff and subjects' awareness, clarity, and reflection of the program and its purpose.

Sample
We identified a sample of subjects representing eight out of the 22 schools where the program runs, using a purposeful, stratified technique to select a representation of the population we served. Our sample size was 17 Outreach Workers, and from that total, we interviewed nine Outreach Workers. In addition, we selected six guardians of the students at those schools to interview.

Data Collection
Data were collected through two different methods. We held one-on-one Interviews lasting from 45 minutes to one hour in length. Data were

collected through detailed note taking during the interview, and then scribed immediately following the interview to provide a substantive rendering of the interview. Quantitative data were collected through a questionnaire which created additional understanding of the impact of the attendance matters program.

Data Analysis

We applied a four-step model of analysis to each of the interviews. This process allowed us to interpret the meaning and significance of the interview data. Each interview was read through, each with a specific lens of focus. The first inquiry was scrutinized through the lens of "What"? What is happening (thoughts, actions, etc.) related to your research question? What are the points of emphasis? What was surprising, etc.? Secondly, we read through the interview again asking "How"? How are they making sense of the issue? How are they making progress? How are they being drawn to or away from impact? The third read we asked, "Why"? Why are these changes happening or not happening? Why have they been able to make progress or why have they not made progress? Finally, we returned to the Heart Triangle method as mentioned above and asked, "What are they coming to believe"? "What kind of person are they becoming"? "What kind of deeper commitment, dedication, passion, etc. are they grow into?" (Love).

Themes

We then examined the overarching themes that emerged from the full scope of our data analysis to illustrate the primary insights and discoveries. This insight and discovery process helped elucidate some key findings which are explained in further detail through the findings. These findings helped our department define some key impacts, both intended and unintended, which included understanding the importance of relationships and insight into caregiver/parents' role in their child's success in the Attendance Matters program.

Quantitative Data and Analysis

As described, we designed a questionnaire to collect data on our quantitative indicators of impact. We administered this instrument to 41 total subjects, including 17 Outreach Workers and 24 parents. The data were analyzed primarily using measures of central tendency.

Intended Impacts

As stated earlier, Community Schools Partnership has six intended impacts that serve as a guidepost to bring intentionality in all our programs. Using these six impacts as a guide, we worked to reduce, as well as simplify and clarify three focused impacts for this flagship program.

➤ Students show up to school on time and will be ready and motivated to learn.

➤ Students will feel safe and connected.

➤ Students and families will develop resiliency and increase independence.

Findings

Finding 1

"Know Your Role..."

The AM program is a necessary component for improvement of student attendance. The focus of this program is to reach out to students and families and give them strategies to improve overall attendance at school. Through our research, it has become clear that Outreach staff need more clarity on their role in AM. As one participant noted, "When I shadowed for months, everyone did it so differently, and some people just did not do it...there is no accountability." By knowing their role, it will create genuine intentionality to how they approach their day to day tasks. Intentionality breeds purpose and purpose will be a platform for them to grasp how they play such an essential part in the lives of the students and families when it comes to matters of attendance. For example, if a child arrives late to school by 20 minutes, three days a week for 10 months (40 weeks), they will have missed 40 hours of class time, which translates to 7-8 days actual in-class time. As OW's, knowing this simple statistic and in their role in walking the parent through these numbers, the parents will learn to understand the impact of their child coming in late.

This is a hard analysis to hear, but one that reveals a perspective that shines a light on a lack of clarity of roles and responsibilities, or, an apparent disregard for them. Typically, when a new staff comes on board in our department, they shadow various staff to get a glimpse of and learn more about the different programs including AM. Each school and each staff member differ in approach and offers their unique method of tackling this issue of attendance, but if the programs are vastly different or not followed through then either the role is not clear, or there is no motivation to execute the role with fidelity. The AM role does have a great deal of autonomy that goes along with it (as is the Outreach role itself), and it can be easy to do the minimum to meet deadlines, but the day to day responsibilities can be overlooked for various reasons. On the other side, eager staff who want to follow through on the role with integrity may still be unsure about how to use their time effectively because the guidelines may not be so clear or may not have consistent opportunity to reach their goals due to other pressing issues that arise from simply being in a busy school.

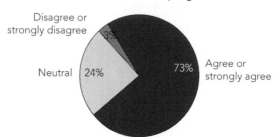

Figure 1. My understanding of the importance of my child's attendance has increased as a result of the Attendance Matters program.

Disagree or strongly disagree 3%

Neutral 24%

Agree or strongly agree 73%

Not all parents are cognizant about how many days their child may be missing from school. One parent aptly described this point.

It opened my eyes. I had no clue she missed that much. I learned how many days she missed at the meeting I had with the Outreach Worker. I said I gotta call my ex and get her in here so we are all on the same page. The Outreach Worker said no problem. I mean she had missed over 60 days. Yea. Eye opening. My kid's education is super important to me. She's here every day. She needs to be here.

Simply stated, the parent, in this case, was not aware that their child was missing this much school. The OW in this scenario, knowing their role, took action to educate the parents for them to make the choices in their morning routine to make these significant changes.

However, it may not always be that easy to keep the role as clearly defined as one would like. There are times during the two hours that are dedicated to the AM shift, that other priorities and pressures from the school asks and situations that pull OW into other school needs. One of the OW observed, "The position is not as cut and dry as 7:30-9:30 am working on attendance. I have had so many students disclose something to me in the morning that interrupts attendance matters because it is a meeting with counselors, admin, and a ministry call." This speaks to the level of trust in and the capacity of the OW's, but it also makes their role challenging to define, as it can appear to school staff that the OW is "another trusted adult in the school to fill needs in the morning and different tasks come up, and attendance matters doesn't always hit the top of my priority list." This is when role clarity becomes essential, not only for the OW but also for school staff. Schools are busy systems and are often not resourced for those 'in the moment' events when OW fill needs and become pulled in other directions that are also important and necessary to deal with.

One of the OW reflected that when working with students who are challenged with chronic absences, "I use that two hours very diligently and focused and don't waste that time, but things come up that need immediate responses." What this tells us is that even though the role may be clear in the mind of the OW, the dynamics of working in schools to support and address emerging and urgent student needs often pulls OW's into many directions. Many of the OW may have the tendency to be pulled away from their role in AM. This is where their role becomes a bit more blurred so while they may still be making an impact in the lives of the students and supporting the school, the focus may not be solely on the child's attendance and developing strategies with the student and family to help deal with those particular issues.

Significance

Outreach Workers' clarity on their role in AM will lead to them being more focused on their task and in their role and give understanding to school staff what their role is as well. Additionally, there are other pressures and needs at the school level that do come up that may temporarily pull the OW away from matters of attendance, but those areas of student need are still important in the overall health of the school and individual students. The data indicate that the importance of this finding and understanding of AM and the impact has a positive impact of providing parents with this education and how valuable they find the information. Parents are gaining more knowledge through the relationship built with the OW's, to understand the impact that good attendance has on their children and how consistent attendance impacts their child's future success at school.

Response

> ➤ More staff clarity regarding the role of the Outreach Worker.
> ➤ Research into extending the time allocated for Attendance Matters.

Finding 2

Jerry Maguire: "You had me at Hello"

Recent research has indicated that having at least one adult in the school that students feel a deep connection with improves their sense of belonging and affinity in the school.

> For younger students during elementary and middle school years, a nurturing and caring relationship with a classroom teacher is vital. Connections with warm and accepting teachers enhance emotional well-being, increase motivation, engagement, and success in school for children in early adolescence. They are also buffers for children who are experiencing mental health problems. (Oberle, 2018)

The Outreach Worker is crucial to making parents, and kids feel more attached to the School community. They are seen as a go-to for families.

Families sense a deep care that goes beyond the academic concerns. One parent shared, "I was most excited because of the support. The Outreach staff the most. I feel excited because of staff – especially with the Outreach Staff!" Outreach Workers reach out to them on a personal level or at least this is how it is accepted or experienced. Our analysis indicates that families feel that the OW is there for them and that they are a personal connection and bridge to the school. One parent from a local elementary school expressed this very positively and energetically.

It is clear that the relationship with staff is one of the critical features of a child's 'hook' to the school and school community. One parent observed,

> The Outreach Worker comes to talk to my daughter to encourage her to come. They have been coming to school a lot since being part of Attendance Matters. Not missing so much, but coming very late. Over the past two years, there has been a lot of improvement. They want to come to other school programs, which is good. The Outreach Worker would encourage me, which gives me the strength to do whatever he tells me to do. I take advice from him, and I do it.

This relationship piece is built over time with trust and care, which in turn has a significant impact on the intentions of the parents. In this situation, the parent took the OW's advice and put it into practice, but also helped the parent's internal motivation to support their child better. Research in this area, we find this very encouraging as similar stories are being told elsewhere about the significance of the relationship with the Outreach Worker and the student & family.

The Outreach Workers have a way of bringing children to feel more comfortable in school and to be more social. As one parent described the relationship with her child, "She absolutely loves the Outreach Worker. She's a huge hugger, a serial hugger almost. The Outreach Worker gets lots of hugs. She is becoming more socially interactive. The Outreach Worker and the staff have been working with her to keep her more focused." The staff is good at drawing the children into the school and giving those children a person to connect with before classes start.

One parent commented on how much the OW changed how her child felt about going to school. She said, "The Outreach Worker offered to come walk up and meet me where I parked so that she could walk my son down to be on time. That's pretty cool. I've never had a school staff offer to come pick up my child before to help him get to school on time." The children and family know that there is something different about the role of the Outreach Workers in the school and what this role does to foster improved attendance through building a personal, trusting relationship. One staff mentioned that "as an outreach worker in Attendance Matters we provide a different option than a teacher or Principal. We take on more of a mentorship role, guiding these students but not nagging them. Finding that balance between firm and standing beside them is important." This is a testimony to the trust that is being built over time to allow a parent or caregiver to let their child go with a trusted staff member.

Significance

This is significant because the Outreach Worker provides a unique connectedness to both the parents and the students, often bridging the potential gap between families and school. It could be argued that even if the staff may be pulled in different directions or need more clarity in their role as mentioned in the first finding, the students and caregivers see the Outreach Worker as a trusted advocate in their lives.

Response

- ➤ The Outreach Workers' ability to build strong relationships is key to the success of the AM and positive influence amongst those involved.
- ➤ Though role clarity is needed for school staff and the Outreach Worker, caregivers and students know the Outreach Worker as someone who is they can extend their trust to and is there to support them.

Finding 3

Empowerment to the People

The data have indicated that parents and caregivers tend to rely on the Outreach Worker staff to encourage and challenge their kids to get to school. While this is good and it has a positive effect on the child to reach the goal of improved attendance, through our interviews we have discovered that this day to day reliance also generates an unattended dependency on the Outreach Staff to bring their child to school. Though there were no specific questions asked in this regard, it organically arose through the answers to our questions. It must go beyond this. Self-efficacy will allow students and families to learn to trust in themselves and not rely solely on the Outreach Worker to get the kids to school. Kids and parents are empowered to know that they have what it takes to make consistent and positive choices about bringing their kids to school and establishing a routine that cultivates the ability and desire to wake up on time in the morning.

Some of the parent interviews have illuminated this dependency on the Outreach Staff. As one parent described the relationships,

I usually ask the Outreach Worker and ask the girls to help me with that…I always take advice, but the Outreach Worker is who I go to the most. (Smiles). For everything, I need to go to the teachers or to the Outreach Worker, but I always take their advice. I tell my girls that the Outreach Worker will be here so be ready! I am going to tell the Outreach Worker if you don't get up! The Outreach Worker says he needs you at the school at 8:15 so please get ready!

Another parent reflected on the role of the Outreach Worker this way, "It is like extra helps. If I can't come for some reason, or my kids are giving me a tough time, it is a huge help that there is back up." While this hits on the significance of the level of trust and the impact of the relationship to get the children to school, it does shed some light on the long-term effect of this relationship and raises essential questions. What happens if the Outreach Worker moves on? What happens if the family moves to another school where this program does not run?

If the short-term goal is to improve attendance and get the child to school, this is great news (which it is), and it meets one of the intended impacts of the Attendance Matters program. However, just as significantly, the purpose of the program is to equip the families; students and parents alike, with practical tools and strategies that they can employ on their own to get their child to school or to come to school on their own both in the now and in the future.

Significance

The Outreach Worker provides the encouragement and structure to provide tools and strategies for caregivers to empower them to get their children to school each day. Reliance upon the Outreach staff is not the end goal as the aim is to allow parents to grow in their independence to make the right choices when it comes to their child's attendance. The Outreach Workers, staff and school, will not be there forever, so values and agency need to be supported and self-realized to put into practice for the future (school and work). What this means is that in our training of the staff, we need to prepare them to collaborate to come up with ways to equip students and families with plans and strategies that can become values to act as guideposts for them in the future.

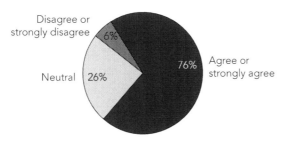

Figure 2. After being involved in the program, I can more effectively deal with issues of attendance as they arise during the year.

Response

➤ Equip Outreach staff with tools and strategies to give to parents regarding attendance.

➤ More direct collaboration with parents

➤ Celebrate relationships and successes!

Finding 4

"Rise up, Routine!" Eat. Sleep. Wake Up. Repeat

Routine is foundational for success for all individuals. It is through routines that children can rely on familiarity and systems to provide a safe space where learning and growth can occur. Routine helps students build strategies in their life so they can make positive choices to come to school. Routine is more than a habit. It also has to become an inherent value. School is one of the cornerstones in a child's life that provides routine and structure. Data show that when children come to school on a consistent basis that they are more positive, engaged and outgoing. This comes in sharp contrast to when they stay at home. Even if kids may think home is more enjoyable, parents and staff report saying that kids are more upset, tired, and distant when they stay at home rather than go to school. Routine and structure strategies are provided for families and students, and as a result, they respond positively.

We all have some routine in all our lives, even if what we have in place may not be wise or have a positive effect. One of the nuances that emerged from our interviews with Outreach Workers we interviewed was the importance of having a routine.

> Having a morning routine. Being diligent with that. Helping them establish a habit, so it becomes second nature. The students tend to get stuck in certain ways and if we are able to alter that and help them get on the right track that is the most beneficial. . . . It's important to stress the importance of finding a routine. We have to do that through repetition. I think they realize the importance but don't know or comprehend the idea of statistics. They hear them, but it is important to stay consistent with this.

Whether we take the same route to school or work, have Taco Tuesdays or choose for the corner table when we go out for dinner, routines are in place to build a certain rhythm into our day and offer some security about what to expect.

This is insightful. "Students get stuck in certain ways…" What he is referring to here is that a student can get stuck in specific 'routines' that have a negative consequence that a child can't to get to school on time or at all. What he is saying here is that if they are able to replace or alter those habits with those that are more constructive, then change can take place. The challenge is that this requires a commitment on the Outreach staff to follow up and check in to see if and how the student is making progress. If repetition is key, an investment of time is needed to start to bring about lasting change in one's routine.

Whether you are taking a stroll through the park or planning to do a 15-kilometer hike, both journeys begin with one step. To start to instill habits in the lives and minds of these young learners, you have to lead by example. If you want to establish long-term values and routines in the lives of the students, it has to begin with modeling the behaviour that is desired for the youth to replicate. One staff member stated, "We provide a morning routine for them. In hope that kids mimic that morning routine, they have their alarm set in the morning. Kids are getting ready on their own." Another described, "I think they learned the importance of having a routine. Having a consistent bedtime is important for them, and I think they now see the importance and that it helps them get to school…they start to understand or know that their body better when they are well rested and that they have the energy to focus." It appears that parents (and students) will learn to see the importance of the routine as they experience the benefits of it.

Each morning the kids walk into the same situation. Breakfast is being served, there are games, books, and other activities on the tables and they generally know what to expect. Even on certain days of the week, students learn that on Monday, Wednesday and Friday they will have time in the gym and that on Tuesdays and Thursdays they will have a hot breakfast. They learn to expect these things on certain days. Modeling this routine of expectation creates security for the kids, and they see the benefits of routine each day when they walk into the program.

In our interviews, it is clear that some parents recognize the value of routine both in the lives of their children and also in their own life. One of the parents observed,

He gets to actually wake up. The morning just offers a different structure. This allows me to communicate with him in the morning and allows him to communicate with others because he has taken the time to relax and wake up fully before school. For me, if I get to say it, I get a little bit of extra rest, and that is great. If I get him here early for morning program, then I get to head back home and steal an extra 10 minutes of rest for myself, and that's wonderful.

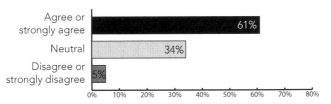

Figure 3. I have noticed a positive change in my child's ability to wake up on time since they started the Attendance Matters program.

Our quantitative data also supported the idea that routines in the program are resulting in changes in behaviors and practices in other contexts.

Everybody benefits from healthy routines, and the long-term results are significant.

Significance

Establishing routines are foundational for successful school attendance. Outreach staff shows and teach parents strategies that they can implement into their daily rituals to make their children ready to succeed, go to bed on time and wake up on time to go to school. The challenge is consistency and building into parents a deep-seated value of attendance, so they learn to do this routinely.

Response

> ➤ Highlight this as a common expectation and language amongst our staff that the element of routine is necessary to speak about and model with families and students.

Finding 5a

The Value of Positive Conversation

Communication is a level of support. As such, parents value communication with the OW. Consistency in positive communication is important, and it impacts parents on a positive level as well as is a platform for staff to continue to build relationships with parents. On the one hand, there is a lot of positive communication that occurs between the OW and parents and children where the OW the level of trust through encouragement, empowerment, and positivity. On the other hand, despite the tenacity of the OW, parents may be unwilling to change their habits because they may feel pestered about this ongoing issue of their child's attendance.

One Outreach Worker who has had many conversations with parents regarding their child's struggle with attendance describes how they try to show up.

The approach that I have used is always not you are wrong, I am here to help, and the school will call and won't get answers but

> I will call on my cell phone, and they will answer, and they will answer right away. Building trust, I will never yell at you. If you have a how can I help you approach, they will open up to you, and we can start a new week together. Allowing people to start over.

This worker's ability to speak into the lives of the caregivers is based on trust and a received experience that the relationship has its foundations rooted in the consistency of connection and a willingness to help rather than to point fingers. It is critical to see that each new day, each new week of school is a clean slate for caregivers and students to start again.

Some parents are open to communication and prefer the direct communication even though it may reveal something that needs to be addressed. Direct communication may also reveal the reasons why there is a struggle with absenteeism and truancy. Through caring conversations, some of these factors are brought to light, which enables the trained OW to deal directly with the situation and offer possible solutions and effective methods of approach. One parent aptly observed,

> The fact that (the staff) communicated with me directly was great, I loved it. She communicated directly with me and told me what she was noticing and showed me (my son's) attendance and then asked what was going on and what she could do. I told her the situation I am in, and she validated me and understood then provided me with options I didn't know about. She told me about all the things going on at the school like the breakfast program. And I've already said it but the fact that she was willing to walk out to my car and meet me, that's pretty cool.

It is clear that in this particular instance that this parent valued communication and viewed the Outreach Worker as someone who has the best interests of the child in mind.

Significance
Communication is the first step to building relationships between parents

and outreach workers. If done positively, this communication becomes highly valued by the parents and outreach staff. Through this relationship building, technique trust building can occur - allowing parents and outreach staff to have more profound and meaningful discussions. For the positive aspects that are affirmed regarding the value of positive communication and conversation, challenging a 'tough' communication also brings new truths to the surface that may be more difficult to navigate through.

Response
> Parents value communication with the OW
> Direct communication that brings difficult issues or personal struggles to the light may be met with more resistance but will help the OW come up with more specific solutions or direct them to the proper resources.

Finding 5b
The Value of Challenging Conversation

While communication is necessary, it can sometimes lead to tough conversations where parents reveal new barriers and challenges including their unwillingness to accept support from the Outreach Worker or school community. One parent shared candidly, "Days can be tough, and I just tell my kids to stay home because it is too hard (to send them to school)." One of the Outreach Workers described, "Some kids want to come, but parents don't want them to go." Another observed, "I have a family where the Dad pulls the child out early almost, and the child wants to be at school but doesn't have control over that. This often creates a divide between parents and students." Despite the tenacity of the Outreach Worker, parents may be unwilling to hear new strategies because they may feel pestered about ongoing issues. There could be a variety of reasons for this such as a previous negative experience or even indifference.

This challenge became clearer in our interviews with the Outreach Staff. In response to a question that centered upon what about the

Attendance Matters program that is difficult and challenging, it was stated. One staff shared, "The struggle between staff and parents and the parents accepting support. My ability to communicate resources offered to parents. Explain what my role is. I want the parents to understand who I am, why I do it and have education on it…parents are tough." In some cases, our data have revealed that some parents and caregivers do not want to accept the support from the OW. It could come down the Outreach staff's ability to accurately communicate the resources available to the parent or the role of the staff member, but it seems that in some cases it could come down to the willingness of the caregiver to accept the support.

Other factors come into play as well. One staff who was interviewed observed,

> The timing of it is the struggle. We can make the calls, but if we are off shift, we can't connect. By the next day, the problem is somewhat shrugged off. The day of (the incident) is more impactful and critical for timing if you want to deal with it effectively. Overall it is a collective effort; parents feel like they are getting nagged on by Outreach Workers and Secretaries. We need to be understanding of the issue but not condemning them. Parents get flustered.

Conversations of this nature can be quite sensitive. If a parent is getting multiple phone calls during the week or month about the same issue parents can begin to feel pestered. One staff gave voice to this reality, "I don't want to be a source of strain on them – to have negative conversations or give ultimatums with parents. To keep communication positive."

Coming from a place of understanding and grace rather than condemnation is key though in moving forward to at least keep the lines of communication open for future conversations.

Significance

Inconsistent communication practices from a staff level can have negative impacts on future communication. Because of undefined and clear

Outreach Worker roles and practices, parents can have negative perceptions from past experience with staff that when staff changes and new staff tries to connect, they are unreceptive. A clearly defined approach to AM would facilitate more consistent relationship building and communication.

Through reflection and discussion, it was noticed that some of the indicators did not address the benefit of asking the direct question around parent communication with the Outreach Worker and the value of the parent to Outreach Worker connection. However, this came up naturally through the interviews on a number of occasions and as such it was an interesting, revelatory theme in the data that is relevant to include here as part of our overall analysis.

Response
> Parents value a positive, consistent form of communication and welcome it as a source of support as part of a trusted relationship.
> Challenging parents' willingness is going to come with some resistance. This should be something that Outreach staff should expect and be trained in how to handle in a way that is non-judgmental.

Finding 6
When you're happy, and you know it…it means that you decided to go to school rather than stay at home and play Fortnite.

Kids may not want to attend school for any number of reasons, but when kids do choose to attend, the social environment it turns out to be very encouraging for them. They like to hang out with friends and their peers and benefit from this social interaction. Parents and Outreach Staff alike have reported that when students attend, they are often more happy and open compared to when they remain at home.

Through our interviews, it was interesting to unravel the correlation between happiness and going to school and unhappiness while staying at home. The Outreach Worker provides an interesting perspective on the children the next day when they do attend.

> They feel a little more reserved if they miss school. I see this more often. The kids are shyer when they come back if they have not been there for a while. If they are at school, they are more engaged and happy…. More trust develops, deeper relationships and even talking about superficial things like superheroes - this leads to stronger connections between me and the kids. This is good for others to see how I interact with other students.

Of course there can be other factors for some students that makes going to school displeasing, but for the purpose and focus of our study, it became clear that when students decide to stay home instead of making a choice to go to school, outreach staff have reported that when they see the child the next day, they tend to be more distant. This is insightful for parents as they often do not know what their child is like when at school.

There are multiple reasons why a child would choose to stay home and miss out on school, but at its core, they learn to believe that being at home will offer more pleasure or be more fun than if they go to school. From the viewpoint of the staff, if kids have been absent for any amount of time, upon their return, they are more shy. If they continue to come to school, this will increase the opportunity for social engagement. An Outreach Worker observed,

> Students are quite happy when they are at school. Many say they like coming to school – it is a safe place, and they want to see their friends and enjoy being around their peers. There is also consistency seeing teachers, Outreach Worker, and other staff members. With a lack of attendance, they come back, and they are a different kid – the combination of not doing anything at home.

Parents also described the positive impact of attendance. One observed, "I think that you know that they have gone to school and that they enjoy it once they are there. That makes me feels good, right? Makes me want to keep pushing and to do my job." Another described the impact of their children going to school, "They are easier to talk with when they come home." She added later that her kids get easily bored at home. These are quite poignant and again reveal a level of enjoyment that is experienced by students when they come to school on a regular basis and boredom that sets in while spending a day at home.

Significance

Even though children may want to stay home instead of going to school, it is evident from our research that kids are often more reserved and disengaged when they return to school after a period of absence. When they are in the school setting, it is witnessed that students are happier. The well-being of the students is healthier when they are in school as opposed to being home. What we found during the analysis of these interviews, what was reported from the Outreach Workers and the parents was that students were happier and engaged when they were attending school.

The reflective and anecdotal narrative (as shown as detailed above) explains the significance of the Outreach Worker and the connection to students in school. What was also discovered was that there was not a statistically significant quantitative support of this finding. Further discoveries and questions would need to be explored to assess the happiness/enjoyment of school as it was not necessarily an indicator we measured in the quantitative analysis.

Response

> ➤ Outreach Workers can use this as an opportunity to highlight this insight to the caregivers for them to be aware of and personally witness for themselves the difference it makes in their children when they come home from a good day in school in comparison if they stay home.
> ➤ A healthy social environment, including both staff and peer group, energizes children and keeps them engaged.

Finding 7

I've got the power!

Parents want to make the right choices for their children but may not feel that they can at times. Independence can lead to weld empowerment as they will not have to rely on the school/Outreach Worker. From the research, we found that when we provided parents with the education and the power to instill strategies on their own, it provided them with a sense of independence. This emerged in our quantitative data as well as seen below.

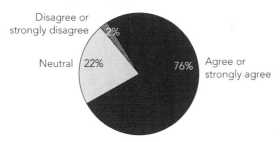

Figure 4. Attendance Matters has made me more aware of the resources that are available for improving my child's attendance.

A vital role for the Outreach Worker is to balance fostering independence and not to build an unhealthy dependency.

As was previously noted, some parents relied on the Outreach Staff to the point of having a dependence on them to bring their kids to school. While this indeed solves the issue in the short term, for long-term success, we endeavour to build the capacity of the parents so that they can operate independently and model this same mindset to their kids for a further continuum of success.

It gives the kids hope...Providing them with tools to feel self-confident and take these characteristics to high school and then to even think about post-secondary in their future. If we aren't involved, who is holding them accountable? We are just herding sheep into high school. We need to be treating kids with more respect and need to deal with their problems now so that in the future they can be determined without us.

Building independence gives the parents and students optimism for their future and resiliency to push through the hard times and bounce back after setbacks. The tools they learn now can have an impact in their future. This also brings a sense of relief and accomplishment to the staff who have been working with the family for any length of time. To see a family who has taken the steps and made the improvements ushers in a real sense of fulfillment that does not have its foundations solely set on the work of the Outreach Worker, but rather the work of the caregiver and student together. Factor in the potential long-term benefits and generational examples set for younger siblings, success in school and career, the joy it brings is very vivid. An Outreach Worker quipped, "How do I feel when a family makes positive development in their child's attendance? Excited! When I stop having to contact them because they are successful now, have made improvements and are self–reliant to get themselves to school. This makes me thrilled." When a family or student moves on from the program and contact with the Outreach Worker in this context and capacity, then it creates the space to reach out to another family with the opportunity to invest.

Significance

Some generational impacts result from this finding. If parents increase their capacity for independence, then they have a stronger ability to teach their children this value. Parents will move away from their dependence upon the outreach worker or school staff to encourage them to get their kids to school and learn to take the situation into their own hands. The hope for the outcome is that children will learn from their parents, and will make the right choices on their own, which will be of significant help as they get older and naturally become more and more independent moving forward into high school and even into their careers. The OW empowers the parents; the parents empower their children who will make attendance and school a priority, which will hopefully be passed down generationally to younger siblings.

Response

➤ It is clear that the end goal is to equip parents and students to be independent and take matters of attendance into their own future.

➤ The generational effect cannot be minimized.

Finding 8
It Takes a Village

Kids need to see that their school is an ally. Families, students, and staff need to "buy into the school." Our interviews revealed that there is inconsistency from school to school and that schools as a whole need to create a culture of attendance where everyone is involved. Schools need to adopt a welcoming lifestyle of participation where students are celebrated when they come to school even if they have been absent for an extended period rather than severely reprimand a child for their absence. All staff, including the school administration and Outreach Workers, should have a knowledge of the attendance resources in the school and utilize them accordingly.

It came up in our interviews that at times some of the Outreach staff have felt alone in their efforts to curb issues regarding student attendance. One described, "It can be a little defeating to stay positive. Also very defeating when the school is not totally on board. I overheard the secretary say AM doesn't actually do anything." There are so many facets that influence this role whether it is the staff grasping their own job description, the resistance of the parents at times and the day to day struggle of the student to make the right choices on a consistent basis. For AM to make the most far-reaching impact, school buy-in is a crucial element to its success and the success of the Outreach Worker. It does not need to be that the CSP staff is swimming against the current or feel that they are on their own. Instead, to have the school in their corner, supportive of their work, will go a long way to generate an encouraging environment for everyone.

In some cases, it lands on explaining the role of the OW and the purpose of AM to the school staff. One Outreach Worker described, "Staff knows what I do, if someone is late they send them to me. The staff doesn't understand the students I should be working with. There are many times that we could be working together with students, but they don't know that I could do those things." Solving attendance issues is not something instantly gratified and takes a village to come alongside a child and caregiver to help them move forward.

When the school environment is positive, and roles are clear the impact is powerful. One Outreach Worker described this.

> I have to say we are pretty fortunate at our school. Staff are quite welcoming and accepting of students' differences and stories. There are a few teachers that get fed up. They are burnt out and lose their empathy for the student that is missing so many days. So their relationships have struggled. Our principal is empathetic almost to a fault. She cares so much about the students that when I talk about needing to get a student to school, she says, "On their own time."

Schools are very busy and have volatile environments where a lot is going on, and things can change quickly. There is a lot of pressure on staff, and not everyone has the same capacity. As schools and staff rally with and around one another student support is always in place.

Significance

Schools may differ in approach, but culture and buy-in are essential. This may connect with the role of the Outreach Worker being more defined and more explicit (Finding 2). A structured and clear uniformed approach would bring more consistency to the program as a whole and facilitate buy-in from the grassroots level (CSP staff). Only when that is established can a consistent school to school-based approach be realized.

This systematic approach of role clarity and understanding of the Outreach Worker impacts students and parents significantly across all departments in an urban district. It is well documented from multiple school districts that the role of Outreach Worker is still in inception as an 'attendance monitoring' role, hence the importance of providing clarity and voice to continue the work in attendance monitoring.

Response

> A positive School Culture of Attendance is critical.
> CSP can communicate the purpose of the program to clarify the role of the outreach staff with more intentionality.
> The well-being of staff should also be a priority, and there needs to be a consistent system of supports and resources in place.

Finding 9

Where Everybody Knows Your Name

Before we go into the details of this particular finding, it is worth noting that findings 8 and 9 do have some striking similarities. Our thought process to formulate two findings instead of combining all the data to create a single finding can be likened to taking a photo of an entire mountain range (Finding 8) and then zooming in on one mountain face to see more of the detail (Finding 9). Finding 8 centers on the culture of the school, the big picture, while finding 9 is more about the aspects of relationships from adults to students.

When staff unites to foster a positive and welcoming environment, the data present to us a picture that when a school creates a culture of relationship building and connectivity, it will impact a child's attendance. A parent noted,

Recently there has been more connections. Before my oldest daughter was with the school counselor, but the counselor did not try hard enough. The previous Principal he was more supportive, but now it is not same support now as before, which is most challenging as it is not the same (support) as before. My kids tell staff things, but not much is done at a school level. This does not affect me, but it affects my kids. So I suppose it affects me.

When this occurs, a student will enjoy that sense of belonging to the school. Friendliness of the school staff, peers and Outreach Workers have a positive correlation to students feeling safe, welcome and connected at school.

Personal relationships are everything. To best support our students in school, they need to be drawn to the school through a genuine connection to the school community. Not only is this draw through relationships with their peers, but with the adults in the school. Without that sense of real connectivity, it remains a challenge for students to seek that connection on their own volition on a continual basis. Without that social network, students will start to feel isolated, which may contribute to their absenteeism. When school staff model the desired behaviour and outcome of engagement it provides a foundation for kids to be attached to the school as a whole.

One Outreach Worker observed, "The School Culture needs to change. The foundations of school culture need to value the impact of attendance and everyone's role in attendance. School needs to be fun and engaging. All staff who smile, care and build connections with kids will see increased attendance and engagement from their students." Students and adults alike sense whether the school values a welcoming environment. If staff are indifferent and do not practice a welcoming demeanor, it could jeopardize student engagement and buy-in. One staff described the key component this way, "The main secret to getting kids to school is building a relationship with them, and then they go and tell their parents, and now you can call them, and they know who you are... that will allow them to make other connections with staff." When a school is supportive, welcoming, and cultivates relationships, staff and students will thrive and will want to invest themselves in their school.

Through our research, some parents have expressed that the school is one of the only places where families have a place to connect with others. For various reasons, they may not have that system of support that many people take for granted or assume. Community for them is found in the school. Or not. How our staff and how the school welcomes and accepts families will impact them in positive or negative ways, so the goal is to have a school that creates a safe and caring environment. The Community Schools Partnership OW plays an integral role in this since they are often one of the first people that kids see on site each day.

As one parent described, "It is nice that he is building connections with other adults outside of parents. I don't have any family, and my husband is really short with people so (my son) is learning the idea of relationship building with school staff. What is challenging for him is the overall respect he gives, he seems to test people and their relationships." This parent gave voice to the importance of the students building relationships with adults in the school even though she feels that her son may not have a sound basis from home to learn from. She notes that her son tends to test people at school and this is the crucial point where staff needs to persevere through these so-called tests and treat the student with the respect they wish him to exemplify even if it may not be reciprocated.

School staff has an incredible opportunity to teach their students what healthy relationships look like. As the whole school lives by this philosophy, students will witness connection become incarnate in every classroom, every break and in the hallways. It can be challenging of course when students give a little push back and test the boundaries, but the results over time will be beneficial in many respects.

Another interesting conversation took place with a parent from a school where she describes in great detail and passion the influence of a teacher on her daughter and what this means to her.

They learn about education and the value of teachers and the help they give. Sometimes they don't feel comfortable to talk with teachers at times. Sometimes the class is too loud, so she comes home upset, but we can't change the class. I have learned about the importance of teachers even though I don't know too many of them. But they do respect me and my kids and they smile and ask simple questions like, "How are you?" I have learned that they are very friendly and approachable. This changes what my child believes about positive connections because of, for example, Ms. X. My daughter loves her. She always helps her. My daughter feels she can talk also with the Outreach Staff... My daughter was abused by her dad, so it was hard for her to come to teachers...good teachers bring her out a bit more. She likes to be quiet, but she is opening up more. This has changed me to believe that school is there for me and for my kids.

This open and honest reflection from this parent paints a picture of the power of teachers and staff. Simple questions that show care, timely smiles and the ability to 'bring kids out' can go a long way to create a comfortable environment for the child and caregivers.

The message is clear. Schools need to come together to be a place where kids know that they are there for them. In this case, because of a family situation, school staff played such an essential part in her feeling comfortable in the school and her opening out more as a student. One Outreach Worker described further,

They understand that there is school staff support. The staff needs to continue the positive environment created. Having a positive climate in the morning allows them to enjoy school. Having a connection to the school is important....I have a few students that aren't in the breakfast club or AM but just come in to say hi to me and the staff who are there because it is a welcoming environment. Students depend on those social interactions. I definitely think that building a good relationship with me helps blossom into other relationships. If I am not there they still feel comfortable coming because there will always be someone else there that they connect with.

We should never underestimate the power and influence of a relationship from an adult to a student, and we may not always know the history and background of where a student comes from.

Significance

When students feel more welcomed and safe at school, they show more desire to attend school. Families appreciate healthy relationships with school staff. The quantitative data in our study supported the value of this fact for parents.

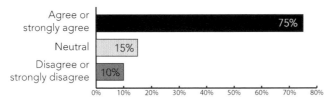

Figure 5. Since being involved in the program,
I feel there are more people at my child's school
who really understand them.

It was evident from the data that a focus on building these relationships creates more of a supportive environment and community culture.

Response

➢ Adults in the school are looked up to. If school staff is welcoming it creates an opportunity for children to open up because they feel more comfortable.

➢ Connectivity to a school will be a factor to keep kids engaged to a school and to help reduce absenteeism.

➢ Parents and children will sense if a school has a welcoming environment or not.

Finding 10

Your Daily Horoscope: Are you missing out?

Our research reveals that students who struggle with attendance show negative impacts in their academics, their emotional state, and with their behavior; Students who regularly attend school keep up with their peers academically, are engaged and happy and can display positive behaviors more frequently. Parents and Outreach staff have both expressed that once the kids are in school, they are more involved and connected to their peers but also they are on track with the rest of the class academically. Good attendance helps them to not fall behind in class where they always have to play catch-up with the rest of the students. Attendance can have a direct correlation to their success in school. Further afield, some parents believe that if they do well in school, their kids will do well after school in terms of finding a job, being successful, or going to college or university.

Getting behind in school work leads to kids not wanting to return to school out of a heightened level of anxiety and are slow to warm up again when returning to class after a long break. The parents we interviewed see this connection, and thus it can create motivation on their part to encourage their children to go to school regularly. One mother described, "I talk to them about coming to school because if you don't go to school, you cannot have a good job. You have to go to school because it is something we value as a family. We value attendance because it leads to success (spoken very affirmatively). I learn to trust the school because they want me to succeed." This has to be a value that the parents or caregivers hold close and emulate to their children.

On the contrasting side, if it is not a value, children may internalize this as a value and learn that school attendance is something of an option and may not necessarily see the impact that it could have on their future. Some students push against that and do their best to get to school or elicit the help and guidance of a staff member or Outreach Worker to help solve this issue. One staff described one student who "...seemed motivated to come to school but she was almost disheartened because she knows that it's not her fault for not getting to school but her mom's. When she comes back to school, she talks to me about how she missed something really cool and understood that when she is at school, she gets to do cool things." Outreach staff described the challenge for students who were motivated to come to school, but whose parents did not necessarily share this same value.

Students may value their education more than their caregivers in some cases. When students are resilient and make the choices to come to school to learn and grow, they will reap the benefits later in life. One staff described the potential impact for these young people.

> (Attendance) And being on time equals better grades, which equals better self-worth and feeling better about themselves. More positive and therefore they put themselves out there more and try new things. They don't put themselves down but will push through hard times – "There is no stopping me now!" Students learn to make decisions on their own and are more independent. They make choices on their own, not me (as an Outreach Worker making that choice for them). I have made choices on my own and earned it.

Some parents may share the same value or learn to accept it as a value, and though they may struggle at times to get their children to school on a regular basis, it is something they are working through with the Outreach Worker or other school staff. Children who are pushing against the will of their parents may face more difficult challenges along the way. But they can overcome these hindrances through the knowledge that school is of benefit in so many ways in the present, but also for their very own future and well-being.

Significance

Creating a school environment through one on one relationships that are welcoming, encouraging, positive, supportive, and makes both the students and parents feel safe is paramount to reassuring regular attendance. When students miss school regularly, it has a profound effect on more than just their academics, but also socially amongst their peers and their willingness to participate. Caregivers are the key to getting kids to school at the elementary level. If there is not a value set around attendance that the parent has, it will be up to the child to take it on themselves to get to school and remain motivated to do so. If staff are observant and have a trusted relationship with the student, they can step in and be an advocate for the child and help them help themselves to find the resiliency to keep pushing when they feel they are on their own.

Response

> ➢ Never underestimate the tenacity of students in their desire to come to school. Assume that they want to go and be persistent with those who may resist getting to school.
> ➢ Staff should work with students to come up with solutions and problem solve to give them the tools to implement on their own.

Conclusion and Next Steps

Community Schools Partnership in Surrey is one of many supports that students have in schools. The Attendance Matters program targets students and families that struggle through chronic absenteeism, and it remains a program that is rooted in trusting relationships with families that serves as a launch pad to encourage and equip people to come to school on a regular basis to decrease absenteeism and become connected to the school through a welcoming environment.

Perhaps many of us reading this grew up in a home environment that always valued education and never wanted to miss a day of school. The desire to go to school still outweighed the desire not to go. Or perhaps you navigated through absenteeism and some of the elements discussed here ring true to home in a very vivid way. All our staff at Community Schools Partnership are in the trenches in some of our most vulnerable schools and communities and come face to face with families, students, and variable circumstances and issues that manifests itself through chronic absenteeism. Maybe you are on the battlefield as well in your community or school. Our hope is that our research has allowed you to gain some valuable insights that may shed some light on the inner workings of home, students and struggles and what we can do to help welcome and value kids individually and create a place for them where they know they are seen in a place where they are appreciated and feel safe.

This excellent work is not easy. It is frustrating at times. But through our resilience, perseverance, and investment into the young lives that we are in contact with daily, seeds will be intentionally planted and cultivated that will see kids who show up to school on time and will be ready and motivated to learn, that they will feel safe and connected to the school they are a part of and that they will develop resilience and independence that will benefit their lives both today and tomorrow.

Maple Ridge & Pitt Meadows School District (SD 42)

OST Programs at Eric Langton Elementary

Roberta O'Brien, Drea Owen, David Vandergugten

Overview of Organization and Program

Organization

School District 42 meets the learning needs of approximately 15,000 students of all ages in Maple Ridge and Pitt Meadows and are committed to educational choice and an inclusive, local approach to special education. School District 42 Community Connections and Healthy Living department was formed in the spring of 2016. There was a noticeable gap in programming during the Out of School Time (OST) hours outside of daycare/after school care especially in rural areas of the city and the downtown core. We currently offer programming in 13 Elementary schools and 3 Secondary Schools within the district and partner with our cities (Maple Ridge and Pitt Meadows) Parks and Recreation Departments, local businesses and non- profits, offering families low-cost quality programming at their home schools. Our partnerships enable us to provide engaging, fun, exploratory, creative and hands-on opportunities for children in schools identified by our MDI as vulnerable on a variety of the five dimensions measured.

Our OST programs are universally available to all children, and a subsidy program is available for those families who require additional support. We selected Eric Langton Elementary to take part in Project Impact as this school is inner city, has a very diverse population including, off-reserve First Nation children, children with varying abilities, and a broad spectrum of socio-economic families.

Description of Programs

Community Connections and Healthy Living offers a variety of programming both before and after school as well as the first three weeks of summer break. Programs fall into one or more of the following streams: physical literacy, art and exploration, literacy, leadership, social responsibility, resources for children, youth and families and community engagement. We carefully examined the OST programming at Eric Langton Elementary for Project Impact this past year. Eric Langton is an Elementary (K-7) located in the downtown region of Maple Ridge with a population of 419 students.

We work closely with the Principal and Aboriginal Support Worker to ensure there are no barriers for our most vulnerable families to participate. The population consists of both French and English track classes, StrongStart as well as The HIVE Neighbourhood Centre supporting families within the community. Families who participated in Project Impact enrolled their children in a variety (two or more each set) of programs over the course of 18 months and many utilized our subsidy program.

Intended Impacts

As a result of our Community Schools programming Eric Langton Elementary children:

> ➤ Are socially engaged and emotionally supported.
> ➤ Are thriving physically.
> ➤ Explore their creative potential.
> ➤ Experience support of the school community.

Evaluation Methodology

The focus of our evaluation was to determine if our OST programming department, Community Connections, and Healthy Living, is truly supporting the District to improve student's social, emotional, physical and academic outcomes. We are witness to happy and engaged children, grateful families, supportive schools and invested facilitators in our programming every day but we did not have any data to support what we observed. Project Impact has provided us with the tools to evaluate the impact we were genuinely having.

Over the course of the project we:

> Defined our intended impacts and indicators to support each impact that focused on children that attend Eric Langton Elementary and OST programs. These indicators were then utilized to create a qualitative interview protocol and a quantitative questionnaire.

> Used qualitative and quantitative methods of evaluation to collect and analyze our effect on social, emotional, physical and academic outcomes of children attending our programs.

> Identified our findings.

> Created responses to support our findings as we move forward.

Qualitative Data Collection and Analysis

Our in-depth qualitative protocol allowed us to access data to inform us of the results of our programs for participating children and any intended and unexpected findings. We planned to use a purposeful stratified sampling technique to select our representative sample population but decided that utilizing only one stratum - teachers, one Aboriginal Support Worker, and parents of children that participated in more than two after school programs over the course of a year - would provide us with an adequate sample. Our population size was 52 parents and teachers, and our sample was 24, however; only 14 parents and teachers participated. Our interview team consisted of Assistant Superintendent, Community Schools and Healthy Living Program Manager and Early Years Centre (EYC) Coordinator.

We considered the population and decided our superintendent would be the best fit to interview the school staff as the interview could become intimidating to some of our parents. To gather the most thoughtful data during the interview process, we wanted to ensure interviewees were as comfortable as they could be, offering to meet at a coffee shop, their home or the school. The Program Manager and EYC Coordinator interviewed the parents at a location of their choice. Interviews lasted between 45-60 minutes asking thought-provoking questions which both challenged and excited parents. Inviting parents to speak about their child in such a vulnerable and honest way is not always easy. We wanted to dig deeper to see if there really has been a change within their child or family since participating in OST Programming. We asked about relationships, values, health, creativity, and growth which challenged our interviewees to think intentionally about their child/student.

During the interview, we made minimal notes, noting non- verbal cues, highlighted talking points, what wasn't being said and then completed longer, more in-depth notes immediately after the interview was completed. This allowed us to be fully engaged in the conversation and enable us to fully reflect on the conversation.

Each interview was reviewed four times, three times by the interviewer, and a fourth by the interview team. Initially, the interviewer reviewed the interview, then coded subject matter based on the interview, and finally created themes to be addressed by the interview team. Thematic analysis was then used by the interview team to review, reflect, combine related themes and name them. We discovered features, causes, catalysts, new and unintended insights and relationships between themes. The most significant themes resulted in our findings, which will inform our responses to each finding moving forward.

Quantitative Data and Analysis

We took a retrospective approach to designing a questionnaire to collect data on our quantitative indicators of impact. We sent an online questionnaire to all 52 families with children that attended after school programming at

Eric Langton Elementary and had a response rate of 25%. The low rate of return was due to teachers not partaking in the questionnaire as the school year had already completed. Data were analyzed by comparing 'before' and 'after' measurements of specific indicators using a scale of 1 to 6 with one being lowest and six being highest. We incorporated the results of each indicator into their related findings.

Findings

Finding #1
Growing Confidence

Description
Through our extensive interview process, it was very evident that parents noticed a significant increase in their child's confidence in a variety of areas since participating in Out of School Time Programming (OST). Parents spoke of the importance of the programs happening in their school where their children feel safe and able to get themselves to programs. With the support of instructors, students developed a higher sense of self-worth, confidence to communicate and the freedom to creatively express themselves on a level they were not able to before participating in the programs. One parent said, "It's been so great for her and for me and because the programs are at the school it makes it so easy and she is so proud and excited to go by herself. It has been so rewarding for her to learn new skills and independence." Another parent said, "She has learned it is okay to go to a program by herself and not be afraid there won't be anyone she knows." For a child to have the confidence to walk into a room and be completely okay not knowing anyone is a significant feat as this is difficult for many adults!

Our quantitative data confirm this finding as well. Many parents stated that their children feel safer in new groups and settings after attending our OST programs as shown in Figure 1 below.

see chart on next page

Figure 1. At Eric Langton Elementary my child feels safe.

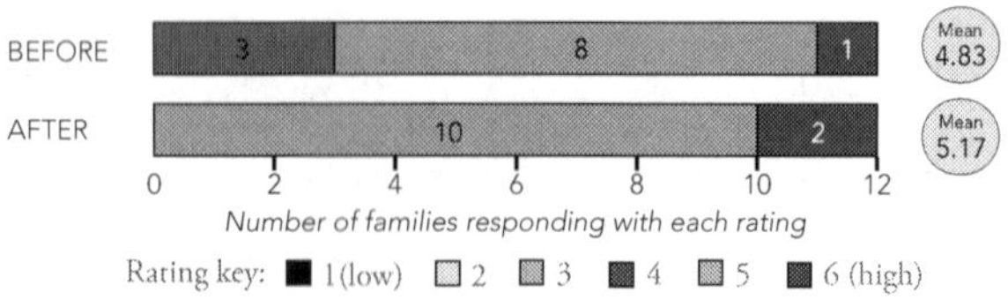

BEFORE   3   8   1   Mean 4.83

AFTER   10   2   Mean 5.17

0   2   4   6   8   10   12

Number of families responding with each rating

Rating key: ■ 1 (low) ☐ 2 ▨ 3 ▨ 4 ▨ 5 ■ 6 (high)

Children feel more confident in their ability to express themselves creatively but also in their daily routine with parents, teachers, school staff and community. Parents also noted that their child is coming home and confidently leading/teaching their family what they had learned in the OST program that day, and they try to instill the new concept into the regular family routine. Figures 2 and 3 below show that children's levels of respect and self-worth also increased as their ability to lead and teach their new abilities to others regularly occurred. One parent stated, "Yoga has really brought out her personality, she wants to show us her Teddy Bear stands, she feels like she has skills that are her own and are worthy of sharing," and, "Her self-esteem is higher than it has ever been. She is very committed to trying new things and asks what's next!"

Figure 2. At Eric Langton Elementary
my child feels respected.

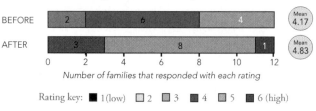

BEFORE   2   6   4   Mean 4.17

AFTER   3   8   1   Mean 4.83

0   2   4   6   8   10   12

Number of families that responded with each rating

Rating key: ■ 1 (low) ☐ 2 ▨ 3 ▨ 4 ▨ 5 ■ 6 (high)

Figure 3. At Eric Langton Elementary
my child feels valued.

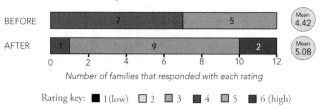

BEFORE   7   5   Mean 4.42

AFTER   1   9   2   Mean 5.08

0   2   4   6   8   10   12

Number of families that responded with each rating

Rating key: ■ 1 (low) ☐ 2 ▨ 3 ▨ 4 ▨ 5 ■ 6 (high)

Significance

We know confidence is one of the main factors for children during the middle years to predict success in adolescence. In the simplest terms, confidence is knowing what you are good at and the value you can provide. Confidence is the foundation for increasing individual's acceptance into social circles and providing a sense of belonging. Our program's supportive instructors have created a safe space enabling children to bloom. Our programs will continue to foster children's perception of self while giving them the tools to excel in their chosen activities.

Possible Responses

- ➤ Continue to support instructors/facilitators with new opportunities for professional growth with regard to child development and SEL
- ➤ Providing opportunities for students to "teach" their skills during instruction time or program time
- ➤ Nurture new relationships students create with peers

Finding #2
Finding a Voice

Description

Developing skills and translating them into all aspects of children's lives, including communication and listening skills, is incorporated into OST programming in a variety of intentional and, most commonly, unintentional ways. Our program facilitators build connections with children which enable them to become more active listeners and effective communicators among their peer group, school staff, family and community members. Many children were described as "wallflowers" or "invisible" by parents as their behavior and disposition did not attract attention negatively or positively, however; through positive and fulfilling interactions with children and adults, OST programming provided those children an opportunity to find their voice. Our qualitative data showed that adults at home and school noticed children that participated in OST programming were more apt and willing to share the knowledge they gained in various programs and mentor others. Figure 4 below shows that parents felt their children's ability to appropriately communicate with others increased significantly after their children participated in our OST programs.

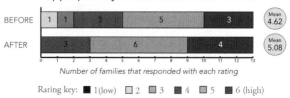

Figure 4. At Eric Langton Elementary my child can appropriately communicate with others.

Number of families that responded with each rating

Rating key: ■ 1 (low) □ 2 ▨ 3 ■ 4 ▨ 5 ■ 6 (high)

Children developed a better understanding of themselves by exploring new activities after school. One parent explained their child learned the communication skills to deal with children of various ages and this "ability to communicate effectively" broadened his self- confidence to develop new relationships in different contexts.

Significance

Many students were not able to speak up for themselves before participating in the OST programming or would let others speak for them, but by building their confidence, they have found their voices and are not afraid to use them to stand up for themselves or others. Providing a safe place to learn and build confidence in their abilities enabled them to find their voice and express their needs and creative desires in appropriate ways to adults and peers. Children's level of communication skills post OST has fostered new friendships with other children of varying abilities, ethnicities, and ages.

Possible Responses

> ➤ Allow more opportunities for children to connect with each other during program time (free play time)

> ➤ Encourage facilitators to find ways to draw shy children out of their shells
> ➤ Ensure programs are well supported (staffing) allowing facilitators time to devote one on one attention to students
> ➤ Provide time and space for students to lead an activity, for example, a group game they learned, an art project or yoga break during recess and lunch
> ➤ Mentor active listening skills

Finding #3
Growing Relationship Skills

Description
Developing healthy social and emotional skills is imperative for children during the middle years to set them up for success as they transition to High School and beyond. OST programs create welcoming places for children to explore and practice these skills. The non-competitive structure allows for all skill levels to participate and cheer each other on as facilitators demonstrate what a caring relationship can look and feel like. One teacher said, "Students that participated in the programs seem to have more empathy toward their fellow students." Our interviews with parents and teachers showed that OST programs reinforce the assets being taught in the classroom and at home by ensuring all children practice kindness, offer opportunities to shine and to lead. Figures 5 and 6 below show how OST programs at Eric Langton have fostered empathy and kindness in participants as is evident by the increase in empathetic and kind behaviours at the end of the programming year.

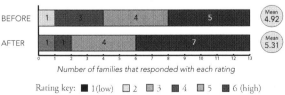

Figure 5. At Eric Langton Elementary my child can show empathy toward others.

Rating key: ■ 1 (low) ☐ 2 ▨ 3 ■ 4 ▨ 5 ■ 6 (high)

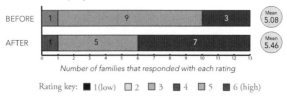

Figure 6. At Eric Langton Elementary my child can display kind behaviour toward others.

Parents also report that because of the nurturing character of the instructors/facilitators their child has been able to gain confidence regarding relationships with adults. Many children shy away from adult interactions, and our OST programming has supported children to build their confidence to not only trust adults but to welcome their interactions. One parent said, "She is pretty quiet and timid around adults now she isn't scared to ask them things." Another said, "She has learned to connect with adults, she loves the Yoga instructor and looks forward to seeing her every week."

A parent stated, "You help someone who needs help. You don't walk past someone who is crying, and you do your best. I just want my kids to be nice people, and that is what I see from Red Fox (OST Program) while a teacher explained, "In the regular school day kids are primarily with their classmates, same grades, and language stream. Our programs invite a range of ages, abilities and language streams together." As the development of social and emotional learning is integrally part of our OST programming, it was extremely satisfying to find that our qualitative data informed us that parents felt these areas of learning dramatically increased at the conclusion of our year of programming. Figure 7 shows that most children fell within the 'high' range of helpful behaviours post OST. Figure 8 demonstrates that children are more aptly playing appropriately together.

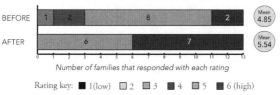

Figure 7. At Eric Langton Elementary my child can be helpful to others.

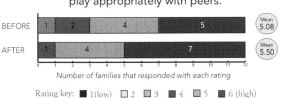

Figure 8. At Eric Langton Elementary my child can play appropriately with peers.

BEFORE — Mean 5.08
AFTER — Mean 5.50

Number of families that responded with each rating

Rating key: ■ 1(low) ☐ 2 ▨ 3 ■ 4 ▧ 5 ■ 6 (high)

Significance

The opportunities that our OST programming offers to the diverse range of ethnicities, socioeconomic status, and abilities of children attending Eric Langton Elementary has created a healthy environment, in and out of programming, for children to foster healthier and more satisfying relationships across genders and ages. Supporting and fostering new relationships between children and adults has shown positive social and emotional results for children. Continuing to support and encourage the social and emotional health of children through a diverse range of program offerings is imperative to bridge communities of people together.

Possible Responses

➤ Continue to offer multi-aged programming
➤ Develop and offer a leadership OST program for the senior students
➤ Continue to work with school staff to ensure students who are finding it difficult to maintain friendships are being registered in programming
➤ Invite community members to be special guests in programming

Finding #4

A Place to Belong

Description

During the middle years the overwhelming desire to belong to "something" or "somewhere" takes hold of children's heart and mind. Through our

OST Programming, we have found that participating students have a heightened sense of belonging than before they participated. Belonging to a peer group or social group is very often difficult for children, and many do not find their place in the classroom or on the playground. A teacher explained, "A boy who is very interested in the building found his niche in the Bricks For Kids Program." OST programs give children the opportunity to belong, to find their place, to find their tribe.

Many children are given a specific role in programs, such as helper or taking attendance, to encourage leadership skills, while others are satisfied by participating in a non-competitive environment that allows them to contribute without any expectations. Facilitators take the time to know their strengths, remember what they like and don't like and use these details about children throughout the program. They also take the time to reach out to the kids who are having a difficult time, either giving them a job to do or sitting down with them. A teacher stated, "Students feel like they belong to this program; if they are not there someone will notice."

As Figure 9 suggests, children are engaging socially with other children and adults far more than prior to our OST programming.

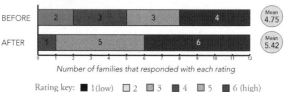

Figure 9. At Eric Langton Elementary my child can engage socially with children and adults.

Number of families that responded with each rating

Rating key: ■ 1 (low) □ 2 ▨ 3 ▮ 4 ▨ 5 ■ 6 (high)

One parent explained, "She doesn't want to do anything she doesn't want to play sports, she tried dance but most classes she would just sit down and not participate. She is now participating and running around and playing games which makes me happy." Our parent and teacher interviews showed us that students who participate in our OST programming find a place to call their own within an eclectic bunch of children both younger and older than each and are given the opportunity to work and play with other children that they might not normally associate with. Not only are children benefiting by these new social interactions, as Figure 10 suggests, but parents are also happy that their child is socially engaged.

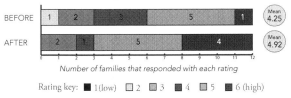

Figure 10. At Eric Langton Elementary my child feels rewarded by their social interactions.

Number of families that responded with each rating

Rating key: ■ 1(low) ☐ 2 ▨ 3 ■ 4 ▨ 5 ■ 6 (high)

Significance

Children developed a better understanding of themselves by exploring a plethora of creative and physical activities offered through OST programming. Children who participate find a place to call their own within an eclectic bunch of children both younger and older than each. Our facilitators are the gatekeepers to this sense of belonging by fostering just the right atmosphere for growth. Children are connecting with many other children and adults and creating a safe place where they belong, regardless of their abilities, age or language. Participants are also learning new skills and gently being nudged to take on tasks that require courage and confidence.

Responses

➢ Create new programs (more variety)
➢ Professional development for facilitators
➢ Share report with teachers to hopefully encourage more teachers to share their classrooms to offer more programming
➢ Continue to ensure facilitators are supported (staffing) for children with additional needs
➢ Parent participation
➢ Family programs
➢ Invite Community Members in
➢ Reach out to local businesses allowing opportunities for students to go offsite for programming creating relationships within the community

Finding #5
New Found Talents

Description

Parents are relieved their children have "found something they love!" For many parents, it has taken months, if not years, to find an activity that their child/ren are eager to participate in. A teacher explained that "the wide variety of programs is important in order for kids to find their interest." The after-school programs at Eric Langton include opportunities for students to create, build, explore and be active. Some programs are group-based, while others focus more on the individual. These programs provide a basis by which children can test whether they want to further expand upon their learnings and skills. Our qualitative data showed that parents are extremely grateful that their children are in love with their new-found talents and abilities.

Our OST programming offers a wide variety of creative and physical activities for children to try. Most are at the beginner's level and offer a fun, exciting and welcoming environment. One pillar of our programming is to introduce a healthy and active lifestyle to children, so they can learn the skills required to play many other related physical activities. When children are confident in their skills, they are more likely to participate in structured sports and take more risks in free play. Parents are stating that their children are choosing more active play based on their participation in our programs as Figure 11 shows.

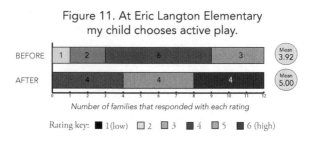

Figure 11. At Eric Langton Elementary
my child chooses active play.

Number of families that responded with each rating

Rating key: ■ 1 (low)　☐ 2　■ 3　■ 4　☐ 5　■ 6 (high)

One parent excitedly explained, "It has taken years to find something she clicks with...she is shy and doesn't much like group activities. Yoga is the first activity that she really enjoys and wants to pursue further. Now she even wants to try some new activities like figure skating lessons". Parents are excited that their children have found passionate extracurricular activities to make use of their time and they are wholeheartedly supporting them in their journeys. One mom explained that her autistic son has "found the varied art programming to be awesome and has found a new passion," and Figure 12 echoes this sentiment as children are openly expressing their desires more.

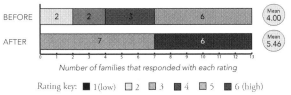

Figure 12. At Eric Langton Elementary my child is able to express an interest in creative programming.

Another parent states, "He now sees himself as a musical artist and not just a learner." She continued to explain that her son has now taught himself how to write music and regularly plays guitar for his family in the evenings. Children are moving beyond expressing an interest in participating in creative activities; they are now seeing themselves as an artist.

Significance

Children are experiencing the gift of potential lifelong, transformative change. Many children participate in many different programs until they find their niche. Eric Langton's after school programming offers choices to children, a plethora of varied programming that is key to support children's development. Children are independently building on the talents and skills they have learned through after school programs, which is also opening new doors to further explore other opportunities and dive deeper into the skills they have already mastered.

Responses
➢ Obtain additional funds through grants to offer more programming

➤ Think outside the box in regards to program planning
➤ Connect with local businesses
➤ Offer leveled programming (level 1, 2 3, etc.)

Finding #6
Cultivating Life Long Passions

Description

We found from our interviews that kids are taking their specific passion to the next level on their own. Teachers have explained that students that participated in after school programs have been exposed to activities that they might not typically be exposed to. Children have been introduced to many creative and recreational types of programming through after school programs, which has enabled them to focus on the activity that speaks to them most. Acquiring music, art or recreational skills and abilities, and building upon that passion has significantly increased their participation levels in the classroom and given them a sense of pride and excitement in creative expression and progression outside of programming hours.

This has been made evident in the classroom as one teacher explains, "Students who participated in the art programs participated in more art activities in the regular classroom," and another offered, "[The student] believes he or she has something to offer now (program skills)." The quantitative data we collected from teachers show strong growth in this area as Figure 13 suggests.

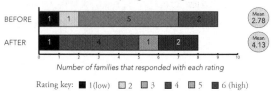

Figure 13. At Eric Langton Elementary my child chooses to practice their ability or instrument outside of programming hours.

Number of families that responded with each rating

Rating key: ■ 1 (low)   ☐ 2   ■ 3   ■ 4   ■ 5   ■ 6 (high)

Parents have noticed that many of their children have acquired an ardent ability to self guide their endeavours and self-determination to explore their creative selves. As one parent points out, "She is taking the skills and teaching others! She is teaching her sister how to calm herself and unwind before bed by teaching her how to meditate." And another parent adds her son now has the "Impassioned ability to self-guide future musical endeavours." The children that attend OST programs at Eric Langton are expressing themselves using a variety of creative mediums and teachers and parents are noticing in their classrooms and at home as Figure 14 shows.

Figure 14. At Eric Langton Elementary my child chooses to express themselves through a variety of creative mediums.

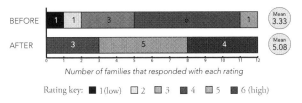

Number of families that responded with each rating

Rating key: ■ 1 (low) □ 2 ▨ 3 ■ 4 ▨ 5 ■ 6 (high)

Significance

Children are developing skills and abilities that they are passionate about. Some children see themselves as a catalyst in the health of others with a deepening value of a healthy lifestyle – taking care of emotional and physical health; while other children are the impetus for their fervent desire to expand upon their musical and artistic aptitude.

Children are now stepping up to the plate with 'something' to offer – showcasing and expanding upon their acquired skills in the classroom; becoming mentors and teachers outside of school, and single handily guiding their artistic talents to the next level. All this suggests that children are figuring out 'what makes them tick' and these desires are becoming embedded in the fibre of who they are.

They are exploring other creative and healthy activities outside of programming hours and expanding their interests into other areas. Our programming will continue to nurture children's interests and encourage them to take on greater challenges.

Responses

➤ Create a once a week student-led lunchtime activity

➢ Offer increased levels of programming

➢ End of the session "reporting" to parents (brag about what they have learned)

➢ Intentional sharing of student success with school staff

➢ Create a mentoring program

Finding #7

Barrier Free Accessible Programming

Description

Parents have expressed much gratitude, while being interviewed, for having low cost, varied programs for children of all abilities and ages, located on school grounds. Teachers have also expressed appreciation and have repeatedly mentioned the more students that can be exposed to these programs the better — especially the families that struggle with poverty and ability issues. We were surprised by the unexpected and overwhelmingly positive comments we received regarding this finding! As we did not intentionally seek comment on this finding, we did not collect quantitative data.

Our programs are offered at school which provides opportunities to commit to a program while parents have the freedom to pick up their children later as children have the confidence and feel safe enough to get themselves to the program without a parent present. "A mother with mobility issues could not get her child to any other outside activity except for the after-school programs," explained one teacher, as the child did not need to be transported offsite to participate in the activity. Another teacher stated, "These programs have exposed our children to activities that they might not normally be exposed to." The low cost of the programs really goes a long way for parents that are struggling financially and the full subsidy program, that is extremely easy to access, eliminates all barriers of participation. "Programs are so reasonable that I can afford to enroll my children in many of them throughout the year," said a parent.

Working closely with the school support staff has made identifying students who require subsidy a seamless venture. Parents quite often don't ask for help even though they need it, having a trusted school employee offer a subsidy directly to them removes the uncomfortable situation of having to ask. One mom said, "All I do is ask my son what program he wants to do, and she [school employee] does it all for me. I don't have a computer, so I don't really know how to register." Our system allows parents to fill out the permission form, register and pay nothing at all. We have a partnership with our cities Parks and Recreation department allowing us to register children and pay the registration fees. So often the bursary or subsidy paperwork is very overwhelming to families and brings with it a sense of failure which we strive to avoid.

District staff and school staff meet regularly to discuss the unique needs of families to ensure we are offering barrier-free subsidizing. Our programs are open to all students regardless of socio-economic status, and the nature of payment is invisible. One parent said, "Programs are so reasonable that I can afford to enroll my children in many of them throughout the year." Parents have also stated they get a break when their children attend the program and don't have to worry about safety issues as the programs occur on school property. A mom explained, "Very convenient for me as I work at another school and don't have to rush here to pick up the kids!"

Significance

OST programming is designed to remove all barriers for children to participate, low cost, right after school, subsidy, as well as, school support to register students. A very high percentage of students were not actively involved in any programming before School District #42 began offering OST Programming due to cost, transportation, and timing.

As we know, parents carry many financial burdens and struggle to make ends meet providing the most basic needs for their children, coming up with additional funds to cover the cost of extra-curricular activities is simply out of the question. Parents recognize the benefits of being involved and carry the guilt of not being able to provide this for their children. Parents can afford to pay for a wide variety of low-cost programming for their children, with complete subsidization of fees available that can be accessed with just a phone call or email, has contributed to the success of after schooling programming at Eric Langton.

There are also no access barriers for parents or children with varying abilities. Extra supports are provided for these children, and of course, special transportation is not required to and from the program as our OST programs are offered in school.

Offering programming at the school, right after school has been imperative for the success of the programming but the children's attendance most importantly. Parents also have the bonus of enjoying an extra hour or two to attend their personal affairs or work schedules.

Responses
- Access grant monies to keep program cost down
- Connect with local volunteer groups
- Parent participation
- School staff led programs
- Connect with local businesses

Finding #8
Reinforced Family Beliefs

Description
Our parent interviews showed that reinforced family beliefs and support are occurring at home as children expand and continue to explore their passions, skills, and abilities. Many families expressed that they are developing a better understanding of health and nutrition as a family unit as children are now guiding their parents in specific healthy food choices they want to purchase at the store and make at home. One mom said, "She understands the benefits of being healthy and wants to improve the health of her family," while another parent explained, "It's great to have what we say at home reinforced." Figure 15 repeats this sentiment as children are making healthier food choices after participating in our programming.

Figure 15. At Eric Langton Elementary my child can make healthy food choices.

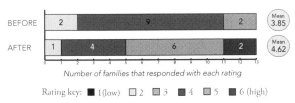

Number of families that responded with each rating

Rating key: ■ 1 (low)　☐ 2　■ 3　■ 4　☐ 5　■ 6 (high)

Some parents also explained that they feel what is being taught at the school and in specific afterschool programs that focus on physical, social and emotional health are the same messages that parents are instilling in their children.

Figures 16 and 17 below shows the benefits that children are exhibiting through creative and healthy activities. Children are more focused when they are engaged and energized to play! A parent explained, "He is asking to go play outside together instead of being indoors." The same is said of creative programming. One parent explained, "I am really happy that my autistic son finally has found another way, through art, in which to express himself." She continued to explain that her son now has a new way to communicate and share joy – he is also eager to develop new artistic skills, and she hopes that he will continue to learn new ways to connect with his family and friends.

Figure 16. At Eric Langton Elementary my child feels focused when learning.

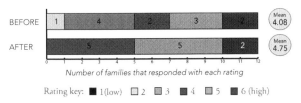

Number of families that responded with each rating

Rating key: ■ 1 (low)　☐ 2　■ 3　■ 4　☐ 5　■ 6 (high)

Figure 17. At Eric Langton Elementary my child feels energized to play.

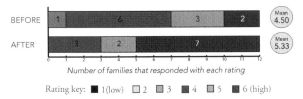

Number of families that responded with each rating

Rating key: ■ 1 (low)　☐ 2　■ 3　■ 4　☐ 5　■ 6 (high)

Significance

Enhanced supportive role exchange has created opportunities for families to learn from children bringing home both new information and ideas, as well as messages that parents are already focusing on. These exchanges give parents more leverage to create further learning opportunities and more experiences with their children. Communicating, planning, creating, working and playing together creates strengthened bonds and connections between parents and children. 0-The added benefits of children being more focused when learning and feeling more energized to play are critical to success at school and in life. Our OST programming will continue to support and encourage families to take an active role in guiding their children's health and creative choices.

Responses

- ➤ Family programming
- ➤ Parent participation
- ➤ Report to parent's student success
- ➤ Family "homework" simple things to do together in the evening
- ➤ Free swimming/skating passes to encourage family play

Finding #9
Bridging to Advanced Programs

Description

An unexpected finding was the depth to which most parents wanted advanced programs offered in our OST programming. Parents explained that their children enjoyed our programming so much that they were taking the same programs repeatedly! Although many children were still happy to attend beginner level programs, many want to explore their potential and growth. An offshoot of this finding is that because there are no intermediate or advanced programs offered, some children have opted to try other activities out of OST programming that they would never have tried if they did not have the opportunity to grow the confidence and skills that they acquired with us.

Significance

Although our OST programming offers a wide variety of programs, we can only provide so many programs a week at each school due to the availability of spaces in schools. We will also begin to work with facilitators to offer more advanced programs to children, perhaps providing some programs at the beginner, intermediate and advanced stages throughout the year.

Responses

> Share report with school staff
> Stress the benefits of OST
> Connect with local business for offsite programming students can walk together to
> Connect with curriculum to validate our programming

Moving Forward and Conclusion

Moving Forward

School District 42 will continue offering quality OST programming within the district and examine ways to expand programming opportunities to other schools. Creating programming to enhance the regular school day using the many resources available in Maple Ridge and Pitt Meadows will be further developed. Reaching out to local businesses, who are experts in their field, will significantly improve the selection and quality of our programs. We have such a varied, array of opportunities at our fingertips that we have not tapped into yet. Our report will be shared within the business community to highlight the benefits to our students, families, and community to evoke a desire to be a part of something greater.

Increasing the variety of programs for children to participate in will continue to support their physical development and creative potential. From our research, it has become clear that we need to take a more intentional approach to encourage local businesses to participate in our programming. We plan to dedicate time and energy in the upcoming year to connect with our local businesses to brainstorm ideas for innovative programming ideas. We would like to explore who is in our community and what talents do they have to share with our students. Including more community into our programming will strengthen the relationships the students have with their school and increase their confidence as they go out into the world.

We also believe that reating a new position in our department would greatly support our schools, students, families, and facilitators with the daily requirements of the programs. A program coordinator would connect with the classroom teacher, parents and program facilitators and be available onsite for the duration of the programs. Simple, caring connections with our most vulnerable students during the transition between class and program by supporting the students in the event they need extra support during the program.

A coordinator would establish the relationships necessary to connect daily with principals, teachers, and parents concerning student participation, success' and ways to encourage them at home. These conversations could significantly impact student success. We have learned that children are open to sharing their knowledge and experiences and if we can improve the communication between home, school and OST programming everyone will benefit. A coordinator would coordinate a Leadership program giving students the opportunity to lead lunchtime activities showcasing their talents, passions and loves to younger students. Students are looking for "more," more moments to be a mentor, more connections and more time to practice their skills.

Sharing both our findings and the findings of our neighbouring school districts will give validity to the work we are already doing within our schools. Educating school staff including teachers, secretaries, custodial and support about the benefits of OST programming will hopefully create more spaces and opportunities for additional programming. Working within the few rooms we have available during the OST time is a barrier as teachers are not willing to share their classrooms for a variety of reasons. Sharing the benefits we have found may inspire a few teachers to open their hearts by opening their classrooms.

The revised curriculum allows for the intentional sharing of student successes between facilitators and teachers while participating in OST programming. Informing teachers of individual growth and development of their students in multiple areas would add depth to their assessments and potentially report different strengths that are not obvious in the classroom. Intentional sharing of information with classroom teachers could significantly impact individual student success. Our vulnerable population, struggling either academically, emotionally or socially, are finding successes within our programming and allowing an opportunity to share these with the family in a formal way would be impactful for both the student and parents.

We have learned that children are looking for opportunities to be leaders/mentors. Developing a Leadership program where senior students can lead activities, be a buddy and share their knowledge, will not only benefit their personal development but also create caring relationships with younger students. The regular school day incorporates buddy classes between primary and intermediate student's and offering an OST opportunity would enhance the great work the school is already doing. Opening the gym or a classroom during the lunch break for leadership students to run activities would create an opportunity for them to shine and increase their confidence, public speaking skills, and engagement with their school community.

Conclusion

As a result of this extensive project we have a few paths, we would like to explore to better support our students and facilitators. We will continue to create opportunities for children to be socially engaged and experience support of their families and the school community by offering quality, low-cost OST programming. Looking at creative and financially secure ways to expand the Community Connections and Healthy Living department will be paramount in our success.

Participating in Project Impact has helped us to understand more fully and deeply what we believed to be the value of our OST programming.

Children flourish when they feel connected, important and valued. Our OST programming is creating space for students to grow, feel and learn. Relationships are being built on shared experiences with peers and caring adults from their community-making room to develop confidence in the fact that they are "enough." Students have the knowledge to share, and if we listen, we can all learn something.

Appendix

Qualitative Interview Questions

New Westminster

What has your child learned [about sports, exercise, and physical activity] during their time with us? How have these lessons changed the way your child sees the role of physical activity/exercise in their mental health? How do they see it enriching their overall wellbeing?

What have they learned about understanding others from being in our program? How have these lessons reshaped the way they see other people? In what ways do they now see the value others bring to their lives?

What have they come to realize better about themselves through the program, and about their ability to manage their feelings? How has this changed how they see themselves in the middle of challenges now?

What have been some of the most significant changes in the way your child interacts with adults? How have these changes made your child's relationships with adults more meaningful?

What skills has your child made large strides in through our program? What skills do they still find frustrating? How does your child embrace adversity in a different kind of way now to overcome obstacles?

What techniques has your child learned to do through the program to stay positive? How is that developing their internal strength and sense of self-determination for the future?

In what ways has being physically active in our program impacted how they feel? Their sense of wellbeing? How has that affected their commitment to being physically active in their lives now and in future?

What has the program done for your child/student's level of confidence? How has confidence helped them strive to achieve their goals?

How has being in this program influenced your child/student's attitude towards friendships and relationships? In what areas does there still need to be growth in attitudes that you've been hoping would be developed by now? How have their relationships become more resilient during times of conflict as a result?

Coquitlam

What have your child's experiences in our programs taught them about the benefits of being connected to others? ➜ How has this changed the way they value developing relationships with peers and adults in their community?

What are some things your child noticed or learned about the perspectives of others (who may be different than themselves) during their time in the program? ➜ How did this change the way they think about the treatment of others? About inclusivity, or diversity?

What fears or insecurities affected your child's ability to participate in afterschool programs? How have those changed over the participation in afterschool programs? ➜ In what ways has this impacted their dedication to engaging fully in the activities they pursue?

What kinds of things made your child feel more welcomed and connected to the people around them in their after school programs? ➜ In what ways has your child become an advocate for these types of programs to others?

What kind of things got your child excited about participating in afterschool programs? ➜ How do they tap into that excitement when they are not feeling good or are bored? How have these experiences changed your child's dedication to ongoing personal growth?

What new skills did your child learn in this program? ➜ How have these new strengths helped your child grow in other areas of life? Where are they still needing growth?

What kinds of things does your child now do as a result of participating in our programs to create a safe and positive after school experience for others? ➜ How did that stretch them to change how they work with others? What are they still working at (or need to work at)?

What comfort zones did your child have to step out of while participating in afterschool programs? What kinds of strategies have they learned to use to manage their emotions when they are challenged? ➜ How did these experiences transform them? How do they now approach personal and interpersonal challenges differently than they did before? How has this affected other parts of their life?

Sunshine Coast

What have you discovered about yourself as a reader from your experiences with us? ➜ How is that changing how you think about reading?

What new books have you read/been reading since coming here that have had an effect on you? What new approaches to reading are you trying out? How has this impacted how much you choose to read? ➜ How has reading become a part of who you are? How is reading impacting other areas of your life?

What books have you found most interesting and enjoyed the most? What emotions come to mind when you think of reading? ➜ How have your attitudes about reading?

What have you learned since coming to our programs about the type of support available to you at school? What's still confusing or hard to understand about how to get support? ➜ How has this affected the way you think about school?

What new things have you tried since coming to our programs to get help when you need it? ➜ How has this helped you in other parts of your life outside of school?

What makes you feel safe to share your ideas in this program? What makes you feel like you can truly be yourself? ➜ How has this made you more dedicated to being the real you inside and outside of this program? What are some of the ways you've been thinking creatively more now than you did before this program? ➜ How has that changed how you think about yourself?

What are some new activities or topics you have explored in this program? ➜ How have these become a part of your life outside of this program? What are you more passionate about since being a part of this program? ➜ In what ways have these passions inspired you outside of our program? How have they shaped what you want your life to be about?

What have you learned you can do when you make a mistake since coming here? ➔ How does dealing with those mistakes make you think differently about yourself? About learning? About school?

What skills do you have that help you participate in this program? What are the things that stop you from participating? What other skills do you think you need to help you? ➔ How has this developed your interests in other areas? How has this made you curious? How are these skills helping you develop other strengths in your life?

What new skills have you developed in this program that have been most helpful to you? ➔ How have your new skills shaped the way you take challenges in this program? In other areas of your life?

Burnaby

What are the significant insights you have received working with Connect Workers? What have you learned about the different ways Connect Workers can support you in planning and delivering tailored programs? How have those insights affected your work in your program? How have you come to view the Connect Worker's role in supporting program delivery?

Since working with Connect Workers, what have you come to understand about developing social awareness in students? What have you learned about the role you play in this type of development (as a positive adult/ service provider)? How have these insights changed how you view the importance of focusing on students' social development in your programs (e.g. encouraging them to be inclusive, demonstrate greater empathy, respect, and consideration of others' perspectives)?

What are some of the insights you've gained from Connect Workers about the best ways to develop relationships with the vulnerable children and youth in your programs? What do you still wish you understood better about developing these relationships? In what ways has this changed how you see the value of forming strong positive relationships with the vulnerable children in your programs? How has this evolved your beliefs about your ability to be a positive impact on their lives?

What new things have you been trying to achieve in your program since you've been working with a Connect Worker? What successes have you had? What challenges? How has working with a Connect Worker changed the way you approach your work? In what ways are now embracing students' needs/interests in your program more fully?

What new skills have you used since working with a Connect Worker to develop program plans and structures? How have you grown and evolved in your program and planning?

What has working with a Connect Worker allowed you to do to support vulnerable children and youth to positively challenge their comfort zones (that you might have not been able to do without CW support)? How has this allowed you to step into your role as a youth leader/mentor/role model?

What is most rewarding about your time in the program? What has been most rewarding about working with a Connect Worker? What has been most challenging? How have these experiences shaped your commitment to the work you do in meeting the needs of students?

What are some of the most rewarding changes in social awareness/abilities you've seen among youth in your programs whom you and a Connect Worker have collaboratively worked with? How has this deepened your passion for promoting social inclusivity among the children and youth in your program?

What are you most enthusiastic about in terms of what is possible for your program where you work collaboratively with a Connect Worker? How do you honour and embrace this and stick to it when it is not always easy?

How has working with a Connect Worker impacted how you feel while working with the vulnerable children and youth in your program? How have your confidence levels changed? How has this developed your drive to continue helping these youth develop through positive, supportive relationships?

Vancouver

Have you solved problems with others in a role as a CST volunteer? What is hard about solving problems with others? What have you learned about how you can solve problems with others in the future?

What have you learned about the differences that people have (skills, talents, abilities, background strengths? How has this changed what you think about differences that people have? How have you had to respond to these differences as a leader?

What has volunteering with the CST showed you about yourself? Has your volunteering changed your ideas about what you want to be?

What problem-solving skills have you learned as a CST volunteer? In what other areas of your life can you use these skills?

Who benefits from your community service? What strengths have you developed as a CST volunteer? Have you overcome obstacles to develop those strengths? Has your volunteering changed the way you see yourself? How might you continue your role as a volunteer in the future?

What skills have you developed being a CST volunteer? What leadership skills have you developed? What would you still like to improve to be a better leader?

What is the best part of being a youth leader? How has this experience helped you with things you are passionate or excited about?

What has been most rewarding about working with groups of people? What is most frustrating about it? How has this volunteer role made you think about helping others/community service?

How does your role as a leader with children make you feel about yourself? What motivates you to keep up your commitment?

Is there anything else you think is important for us to know about what it is like to volunteer with the CST?

Surrey
For Parents

What have you discovered that's been most helpful to you since your child has been a part of the attendance program at your school? What have you learned that's meant the most to you? ➔ How has this changed what you believe about what your child can achieve (or what will help them thrive) in school?

What do you think your child has learned from the attendance program that's been most helpful to them? What do you think they're still struggling to understand? ➔ How have these ideas influenced what they value about school attendance (or being at school)?
How has this influenced what you value about attendance?

What differences have you observed in your child's interests when they go to school compared to when they stay at home? ➔ How has this affected how you value the attendance program/school? How is this helping you to trust in the school to support your child's well-being?

What has your child learned about building healthy relationships with school staff since being a part of this program? What is challenging about building these connections? What have you learned about the importance of your child having healthy relationships with school staff? ➜ How has this changed what your child believes about the importance of making positive connections with school staff? How has it changed what you believe?

What have you learned in the attendance program about the importance of proactive problem-solving in your family's day-to-day life? ➜ How has this changed the way you think about the choices you make for your family? How are you thinking differently about your role as a parent?

What strategies have been used to improve attendance since connecting with the OW? What are the toughest parts about implementing these strategies? ➜ How has this additional structure strengthened your child's ability to make positive choices? How has it strengthened your ability? How has this been impacting (strengthening/straining) relationships in the family?

What have been the most significant achievements with your children's attendance since they have been a part of the attendance program? ➜ How has this helped you develop the capacity to support the child(ren) in other parts of life beyond attendance alone?

What school connections have you and your child(ren) been trying to make? What's been most challenging about this? ➜ In what ways have you and your child grown since being a part of this program that have helped you overcome these challenges? In what ways do you still need to grow to further develop these relationships?

What are some of the most difficult choices you have made since being a part of this program? ➜ How are these choices helping you take control of how you respond to difficult situations? How is this affecting other parts of your life?

What do you think has been most rewarding for your child about making more positive choices since participating in Attendance Matters? What's been most rewarding for you? What have you both been frustrated by? ➔ How do you and your child stay determined during those times? What keeps you both committed to the process?

What about having this support from the attendance program is like a breath of fresh air? What about making those choices has been sucking the air out of the room? ➔ How do these affect your commitment to ensuring your child(ren) get the most out of school?

When have you felt most excited about improving your child's attendance since coming to this program? When have you felt least excited? ➔ How do you keep engaged through those times when you're not feeling inspired?

Surrey
For Outreach Workers

What do you think your student has learned from the attendance program that's been most helpful to them? What do you think they're still struggling to understand? ➔ How have these ideas influenced what they value about school attendance (or being at school)? How has this changed what they believe about what they can achieve (or what will help them thrive) in school?

What differences have you observed in your students when they come to school compared to when they stay at home? ➔ How is this helping the students and their families to trust in the school to support their personal well-being?

What has your student learned about building healthy relationships with school staff since being a part of this program? What do they still need to learn to about building relationships? ➔ How have these types of experiences changed what the students? believe about the importance of making positive connections with school staff?

What have your students learned about the importance of proactive problem-solving in their day-to-day life? →How has this changed the way they think about the choices for their family? How are family members thinking differently about their roles as parents?

What strategies have your students used to improve attendance since being a part of the Attendance program? What are the toughest parts about implementing these strategies? → How has this additional structure strengthened your students' ability to make positive choices? How has this been strengthening/straining relationships between the students and their family?

What have been the most significant achievements with your student's attendance since they have been involved with the program? What have been some of the most difficult choices the students have had to make? →How are these experiences helping your students take control of how they respond to difficult situations? How is this affecting other parts of their life/school?

What new school connections have your students been trying to make since joining the program? What's been most challenging about this for them? → In what ways have they grown that has helped them overcome these challenges? In what ways do your students (and their families) still need to grow to further develop these relationships?

What are some of the most difficult choices your students have made since being a part of this program? How has this gone for them? → How are these choices helping your students take control of how they respond to difficult situations? How is this affecting other parts of their life/school?

What aspects of your student's making positive choices has been the most rewarding for them? What has been the most frustrating for them? ➔ How do your students stay determined during those times?

What about your students having this support from Attendance Matters is like a breath of fresh air? What about the Attendance Program has been sucking the air out of the room? ➔ How do these affect your student's commitment to ensuring they get the most out of school? What is discouraging for your students about interactions with school staff? What is meaningful about these interactions?

When have your students felt most excited about improving their attendance since coming to this program? When have your students felt least excited? ➔ How do your students keep engaged through those times when they are not feeling inspired?

United Way of the Lower Mainland

What has your involvement with the LMOST alliance/ School's Out COP / Summit taught you about the importance of OST? What's still missing or hard to grasp for you about this? ➔ How has that changed the way you think about OST, and your role within it?

What have your experiences with LMOST/ School's Out COP / Summit reinforced for you about the impact of OST on children? ➔ What does this new knowledge mean for (or what has been most meaningful) you and your programming? How has this involvement changed the way you see the future of the programming you offer?

What have you discovered about your role in the collective / regional effort around OST since being involved with LMOST / School's out COP / Summit? ➔ How has this shifted your perspective as an OST service provider working in a collective effort? How is this influencing your thinking about the importance of collaboration in the process of OST development, delivery, and evaluation?

What skills have you developed to help you promote OST programs? What skills do you still need to develop to effectively promote your program? ➜ How is this helping you to become an advocate for program sustainability?

What barriers to effective OST collaboration are you still struggling with? ➜ What inner strengths have you tapped into to overcome those barriers? How has this changed who you are as an OST leader/collaborator? In what ways would you still need to grow to be the kind of OST leader/collaborator you want to be for your community?

What have been some challenges in setting/implementing new program? What have been your biggest accomplishments? ➜ How are you embracing the shift towards quality in your program differently now than you were before? In what ways are you becoming a more reflective practitioner?

What kinds of emotions do you find yourself experiencing most frequently when you connect with your community? What makes you most deeply passionate about your community connections? ➜ How has this deepened your commitment to meeting the community's needs?

What has been the most exciting part of participating in the LMOST alliance / School's out COP/Summit? What's been most frustrating? ➜ How has this manifested itself to action for you? How has it made you more dedicated towards collaboratively supporting OST?

What has been rewarding for you in participating in LMOST alliance / School's Out COP / OST Summit? ➜ How has that changed your level of perseverance to partake in the difficult work reality of OST programming?

In what ways are you more concerned about elements of quality in OST after your participation in the OST summit? ➜ How has that affected your commitment for quality programming?

Thinking ahead 3-5 years into the future, if everything goes exactly as you hope it will, what does your ideal program look like? What does your ideal community look like? How has participating in LMOST alliance / School's out COP / Summit helped you move closer to/achieve that vision?

Maple Ridge

What has your child discovered about creating and maintaining relationships while participating in our programs? In what ways has this understanding changed how they value others? How has it changed how they see themselves (in social settings)?

What has your child learned about nutrition and a healthy, active lifestyle while attending our programs? How do they think differently about the choices they now make? How has this enabled them to embrace healthier food choices and physical activities? In what ways does your child's perspective still need to change for them to be as healthy as you want them to be?

What has your child learned about being creative from our programming? How committed are they to continue to explore other creative pathways? How has this changed how they see their ability to creatively express themselves?

What relationships skills has your child developed since participating in our programming? How have these new skills transformed the quality of your children's relationships with other children and adults? How has this enabled them to grow and develop as an individual? In what ways do they still need to grow?

What kinds of healthy food choices and activities does your child try out or explore now that they didn't before? What areas of health are they still struggling to make changes in? How are these changes causing them to develop in other areas of life?

How have your child's creative skills blossomed since participating in our programs (ie. Drawing, building, dancing, singing)? What have been some of their most significant creative accomplishments? How have these experiences developed their creative identity? How are they continuing to grow and develop through their creative expression?

What experiences has your child had in our programs that have made them feel safe and welcomed or a sense of belonging? How has this developed their commitment to being, kind, caring and helpful (inclusive) to others?

What has been the most rewarding part of learning new skills and behaviours related to a healthy lifestyle for your child? What has changed about their levels of energy and focus? What's discouraged them? In what ways have these experiences changed their commitment to pursue a healthy lifestyle?

What has our programming done for your child's level of creative enthusiasm? What different types of creative programs have they enjoyed? How has this deepened their passion for creative expression? For exploring new ways to be creative?

Manufactured by Amazon.ca
Bolton, ON